» The Regrets

» Joachim du Bellay

The Regrets

A BILINGUAL EDITION

TRANSLATED FROM THE FRENCH AND LATIN

BY DAVID R. SLAVITT

NORTHWESTERN UNIVERSITY PRESS

EVANSTON, ILLINOIS

Northwestern University Press
Evanston, Illinois 60208-4170

Printed in the United States of America

10 9 8 7 6 5 4 3 2

ISBN 0-8101-1993-5

Sonnet 35 previously appeared in *Frigate*.
"To the Reader" previously appeared in *Classical Outlook*.

Library of Congress Cataloging-in-Publication Data

Du Bellay, Joachim, 1525 (ca)–1560.
    [Regrets. English & French]
    The regrets : a bilingual edition / Joachim du Bellay ; translated from the
French and Latin by David R. Slavitt.
        p. cm. — (European poetry classics)
    ISBN 0-8101-1993-5 (alk. paper)
    I. Slavitt, David R., 1935– II. Title. III. Series.
PQ1668.R4E5 2003
841'.3—dc21

                                                                    2003007640

For Laurie and Leon
D.R.S.

» Contents

» Translator's Preface

Joachim du Bellay was born in 1525 at the Château de la Turme-
lière in Liré, a small town in Anjou on the left bank of the Loire.
Orphaned at the age of seven, he was raised by a brother twenty
years older than he, and from what he reports in *La Deffence et
illustration de la langue françoyse*, we know that he wandered
around the Angevin countryside talking with artisans of various
kinds and learning the words they used in several crafts and
trades. In his late teens, he fell in love with a cousin, Olive de
Sévigné, and for her wrote his first sonnet sequence, *L'Olive*, a
celebration not only of their love but also of its setting, that
countryside for which he frequently expresses nostalgia in *The
Regrets*.

When Mlle de Sévigné married someone else, du Bellay,
deeply distressed, was sent off to the Faculté de Poitiers to study
law. One of his friends there was Guillaume Aubert, who would
later be responsible for the posthumous publication of du Bellay's
work. At this same time or a little later, after a chance encounter
at an inn, he struck up an acquaintance with Pierre de Ronsard,
and they became friends and, not long afterward, students to-
gether at the Collège de Coqueret in Paris, where Jean Dorat, the
preeminent classicist, was master. Jean-Antoine de Baïf was an-
other slightly younger student there. These four were later joined
by Rémi Belleau, Étienne Jodelle, and Pontus de Tyard, and they
became the group known first as the Brigade and then later—
because there were seven of them and in an allusion to the seven
Greek poets of Alexandria—the Pléiade.

That the Pléiade poets are not currently a part of the core curriculum of American colleges and universities should not be surprising. Students of French literature are familiar with them, of course, but this is a dismal time for the study of literature and what Walter Pater said of them—in praise—in *The Renaissance* suggests the reason for their present neglect: he refers to "the qualities, the value, of the whole Pleiad school of poetry, of the whole phase of taste from which that school derives—a certain silvery grace of fancy, nearly all the pleasure of which is in the surprise at the happy and dexterous way in which a thing slight in itself is handled."

That "silvery grace of fancy" is not much in fashion now among academics. It is "elitist." It assumes a knowledge of and a love for the classics. To put it more clearly and aggressively, these were poets of aristocratic elegance, mannered and civilized, whose playful performances were intended as diversions for themselves and like-minded friends from whom they could expect a level of cultural poise and sophistication that students and some faculty members these days cannot provide. Their encounter with these works, then, they may find either flattering or challenging and off-putting—depending on the degree of openness and goodwill they bring to their labors. Those who take pleasure in reading Lovelace and Suckling, Pope and Prior, are likely to find the Pléiade poets in general, and Ronsard and du Bellay in particular, amusing and engaging. Those who prefer Wordsworth or Blake or Whitman and who look for fervor, sincerity, and even political engagement may not be altogether comfortable with these bijoux.

Les Regrets is actually a very accessible and charming book. The title is a wry joke, for the reference is to Ovid's *Tristia*, which the great Latin poet wrote in Tomis, on the shores of the

Black Sea, in which primitive outpost he was pining for Rome and civilization. Du Bellay was in Rome, where the decadent excess of court life was depressing him, and he was longing for Anjou and France—but he was also making fun of his own distress, a gesture in the direction of légèreté and good manners.

He was in Rome, after all, working as a kind of confidential secretary to a cardinal, his father's cousin, Jean du Bellay, to whom he had dedicated his *Deffence.* When Henri II sent Cardinal du Bellay to Rome to look after the interests of France, Joachim went with him. While in Rome, in his cousin's entourage, du Bellay wrote *Les Antiquités de Rome,* a series of thirty-two sonnets that are graceful performances but conventional, more or less picture postcards of the Roman ruins that do not exhibit the range and the engaging personality of *The Regrets.*

As a sample of these, I offer number 27:

You who contemplate Rome amazed at its old
pride in a power that rivaled that of heaven,
its venerable palaces, its seven
hills, its arches, baths, its temples of gold,
consider its vistas of ruin, its fields of rubble,
middens of bones that Time has gnawed on so,
which patient craftsmen fashioned long ago,
these sad remains of all their skill and trouble.

Then look again more closely and you may see
how Rome, rummaging through her antiquity,
rebuilds herself with works as grand as before:
judge for yourself whether the Roman demon
can, by an act of strength and superhuman
will, restore these ruins to life once more.

(As a young man, probably when he was still at Cambridge, Edmund Spenser translated this sonnet sequence as "Ruines of Rome," and the mysterious "Songe"—or "Dream"—which follows it as the "Visions of Bellay.")

It was from du Bellay's involvement with the ordinary business of the day in his cousin's retinue that the less literary and poetic but much more interesting poems of *The Regrets* would come. He is confiding in us, or, often, confiding in his friends and inviting us to eavesdrop, about the scandals, the frustrations, the occasional pleasures, the jokes, and the cattiness of his real-world experience, which is vivid and immediate. There is, moreover, a real melancholy—he preferred life at home and longed for his Anjou almost as keenly as Ovid longed for Rome. These sonnets make up a body of work that is wonderfully appealing and oddly contemporary in feeling. The late C. H. Sisson's version of these poems appeared almost twenty years ago, and if I have a somewhat different view of how they ought to be Englished, I agree with Sisson's judgment that du Bellay "is a greater poet than Ronsard." My only qualification would be that, instead of "greater," I'd prefer simply to say that he was "better." Du Bellay makes friendly fun in some of these sonnets of Ronsard's later heroic phase, in which mode he is of only historical interest. Du Bellay's poems of complaint, with their breezy intimacy, their brave dysphoria, and their spontaneity, have a freshness and immediacy that invited my attention and will, I trust, be pleasing to others as well.

There are 191 sonnets in *Les Regrets et autres oeuvres poétiques*, as the 1558 volume is entitled, but more than one editor has suggested that the last sixty of these do not belong to the sonnet sequence but are the "other poetic works" to which the title page refers. These sixty sonnets were apparently written after the poet had returned to France. Sonnet 128 speaks of du Bellay's return to France by sea, probably writing in anticipation of the voyage as Ovid did in the *Tristia*. Then 129 is a fantasy of his homecoming, and 130 is a comparison of his return to that of Ulysses. The three pieces suggest a moment of conclusion, which Sisson notes and with which I agree.

The text on which I have relied is that edited by S. de Sacy (Paris, Gallimard, 1967). I have also consulted Sisson's version (Manchester, Carcanet, 1984), which offers *en face* a French text based on that of the Textes littéraires français (Geneva, Librairie Droz, 1966) edited by J. Joliff and M. A. Screech and the two volumes of du Bellay's *Poésies Françaises et Latines* (Paris, Garnier, 1918) edited by E. Courbet.

» The Regrets

» » » Ad Lectorem

Quem, lector, tibi nunc damus libellum,
Hic fellisque simul, simulque mellis,
Permixtumque salis refert saporem.
Si gratum quid erit tuo palato,
Huc conviva veni: tibi haec parata est
Coena. Sin minus, hinc facesse, quaeso:
Ad hanc te volui haud vocare coenam.

» » » To the Reader

Reader, this little book we bring
is flavored of honey and gall and more
than a dash of salt. Should this delight
your palate, lovely; come and dine.
But should you find it's not your thing,
then leave. The meal was not meant for
the likes of you. It's quite all right.
You go your way, and I'll go mine.

» » » A Monsieur d'Avanson

CONSEILLER DU ROI
EN SON PRIVÉ CONSEIL

Si je n'ai plus la faveur de la Muse,
Et si mes vers se trouvent imparfaits,
Le lieu, le temps, l'âge où je les ai faits,
Et mes ennuis leur serviront d'excuse.

J'étais à Rome au milieu de la guerre,
Sortant déjà de l'âge plus dispos,
A mes travaux cherchant quelque repos,
Non pour louange ou pour faveur acquerre.

Ainsi voit-on celui qui sur la plaine
Pique le bœuf ou travaille au rempart
Se réjouir, et d'un vers fait sans art
S'évertuer au travail de sa peine.

Celui aussi, qui dessus la galère
Fait écumer les flots à l'environ,
Ses tristes chants accorde à l'aviron,
Pour éprouver la rame plus légère.

On dit qu'Achille, en remâchant son ire,
De tels plaisirs soulait s'entretenir,
Pour adoucir le triste souvenir
De sa maîtresse, aux fredons de sa lyre.

» » » To Monsieur d'Avanson

If I no longer enjoy the Muse's regard,
and my verse sometimes seems rough, the time, the place,
the age in which I write, and the burdens I face
may offer some excuses for how it is marred.

I was at Rome in wartime. These were not days
in which a poet could find the requisite
calm he needs for the exercise of his wit
to gain the readers' attention or earn their praise.

What one sees here is the kind of verse you get
from a sunburned plowman or soldier on his rampart
who wants to turn what he goes through not into art
but only an anodyne to the pain and sweat

he undergoes. Or think of the galley slaves
who sing sad songs while they pull on their oars together
hoping to make the oars seem lighter, the weather
better, dragging the heavy ship through the waves.

So Achilles, chewing his bitter ire
and his grief at the loss of the beautiful girl, hummed
a wordless song to soothe himself as he strummed
distractedly sad chords on the strings of his lyre.

Ainsi flattait le regret de la sienne
Perdue, hélas, pour la seconde fois,
Cil qui jadis aux rochers et aux bois
Faisait ouïr sa harpe thracienne.

La Muse ainsi me fait sur ce rivage,
Où je languis banni de ma maison,
Passer l'ennui de la triste saison,
Seule compagne à mon si long voyage.

La Muse seule au milieu des alarmes
Est assurée et ne pâlit de peur:
La Muse seule au milieu du labeur
Flatte la peine et dessèche les larmes.

D'elle je tiens le repos et la vie,
D'elle j'apprends à n'être ambitieux,
D'elle je tiens les saints présents des dieux
Et le mépris de fortune et d'envie.

Aussi sait-elle, ayant dès mon enfance
Toujours guidé le cours de mon plaisir,
Que le devoir, non l'avare désir,
Si longuement me tient loin de la France.

Je voudrais bien (car pour suivre la Muse
J'ai sur mon dos chargé la pauvreté)
Ne m'être au trac des neuf Sœurs arrêté,
Pour aller voir la source de Méduse.

And so Orpheus, too, crooned of his grief
at the loss—Alas! for the second time!—of his sweet
Eurydice, as if the rocks at his feet
and the leafy trees around him could offer relief.

Thus does the Muse visit me here on the bank
of this foreign river, where I live far from my own
house and pass long seasons here, alone,
my only company, whom I welcome and thank.

Amidst the rumors here, the alarums and fears,
the Muse, alone unruffled and unafraid,
concentrates on her labors, sticks to her trade,
never voicing complaints or shedding tears.

From her I learn equanimity and poise
and how to put ambition aside, and I pray,
as the pious do to the saints, that she show me the way
not to envy the pleasures another enjoys.

She also knows my childhood and can intuit
what my solaces are, and my desires,
and that it is duty and not greed that inspires
this labor in exile. (Why else would I do it?)

Sometimes I'd rather not have to follow the Muse, a
goddess who demands one make a vow
of poverty which I have observed (and how!);
I sometimes think I'd as soon confront the Medusa.

Mais que ferai-je afin d'échapper d'elles?
Leur chant flatteur a trompé mes esprits,
Et les appas auxquels elles m'ont pris
D'un doux lien ont englué mes ailes.

Non autrement que d'une douce force
D'Ulysse étaient les compagnons liés,
Et sans penser aux travaux oubliés
Aimaient le fruit qui leur servait d'amorce.

Celui qui a de l'amoureux breuvage
Goûté mal sain le poison doux-amer,
Connaît son mal, et contraint de l'aimer,
Suit le lien qui le tient en servage.

Pour ce me plaît la douce poésie,
Et le doux trait par qui je fus blessé:
Dès le berceau la Muse m'a laissé
Cet aiguillon dedans la fantaisie.

Je suis content qu'on appelle folie
De nos esprits la sainte déité,
Mais ce n'est pas sans quelque utilité
Que telle erreur si doucement nous lie.

Elle éblouit les yeux de la pensée
Pour quelquefois ne voir notre malheur,
Et d'un doux charme enchante la douleur
Dont nuit et jour notre âme est offensée.

But from the Muses, it is not easy to flee:
with their flattering song, they have enchanted my spirit
which isn't my own anymore, for when I hear it,
I'm a bird a fowler has charmed out of its tree.

We read about that legendary fruit
Ulysses' companions ate that made them all
put their duty and honor beyond recall
and reduced them from manhood to absolute

servitude. Such a potion, bittersweet,
has paralyzed my will and poisoned my brain
so that, despite my better self, I remain
in thrall here, quite unable to use my feet,

and scribbling verse. The Muse has taken aim
with her pretty little bow, and I am shot,
not killed but only wounded, and have forgot
those troubles I might otherwise proclaim.

It's madness, I admit it freely, but still
I am content, for if the goddess bless,
we learn that, for all its vaunted uselessness,
poetry can be soothing, and she will

come to our aid, dazzle our eyes, transform
our miseries to a charming parlor game,
redeeming us who labor in her name,
and protecting us from doing ourselves harm.

Ainsi encor la vineuse prêtresse,
Qui de ses cris Ide va remplissant,
Ne sent le coup du thyrse la blessant,
Et je ne sens le malheur qui me presse.

Quelqu'un dira: De quoi servent ces plaintes?
Comme de l'arbre on voit naître le fruit,
Ainsi les fruits que la douleur produit
Sont les soupirs et les larmes non feintes.

De quelque mal un chacun se lamente,
Mais les moyens de plaindre sont divers:
J'ai, quant à moi, choisi celui des vers
Pour désaigrir l'ennui qui me tourmente.

Et c'est pourquoi d'une douce satire
Entremêlant les épines aux fleurs,
Pour ne fâcher le monde de mes pleurs,
J'apprête ici le plus souvent à rire.

Or si mes vers méritent qu'on les loue
Ou qu'on les blâme, à vous seul entre tous
Je m'en rapporte ici: car c'est à vous,
A vous, Seigneur, à qui seul je les voue:

Comme celui qui avec la sagesse
Avez conjoint le droit et l'équité,
Et qui portez de toute antiquité
Joint à vertu le titre de noblesse:

Thus, when the priestess, drunk and frenzied, sings
in cries that echo on Ida, she hardly feels
the thyrsus's blows, for the act of singing heals—
and I, too, know the comfort that it brings.

You may well ask of these complaints, what use
are they, the fruits of a gnarled and twisted tree
that has withstood the winds' adversity?
But see how smooth they are, and taste their juice.

How does a man respond to wickedness?
Some sulk, some fulminate, or pray, or curse.
My choice has always been to turn to verse
to neutralize the causes of my distress.

And this may be why my satire appears
so gentle, with spines and thorns that are intermixed
with flowers. I don't expect the world to be fixed,
and laughter serves my purpose better than tears.

But whether my verses are worth the time they require,
or someone objects that they're not, I appeal to you,
the man of taste and judgment I offer them to,
and the one to whose approval I aspire,

one in whom sagacity is married
to an innate sense of fairness upon which good
taste depends. These virtues are in your blood,
as noble as the title you have carried

Ne dédaignant, comme était la coutume,
Le long habit, lequel vous honorez,
Comme celui qui sage n'ignorez
De combien sert le conseil et la plume.

Ce fut pourquoi ce sage et vaillant prince,
Vous honorant du nom d'ambassadeur,
Sur votre dos déchargea sa grandeur,
Pour la porter en étrange province:

Récompensant d'un état honorable
Votre service, et témoignant assez
Par le loyer de vos travaux passés
Combien lui est tel service agréable.

Qu'autant vous soit agréable mon livre,
Que de bon cœur je le vous offre ici:
Du médisant j'aurai peu de souci
Et serai sûr à tout jamais de vivre.

from the day of your birth. You do not scorn the dark
robes of a judge or professor, but, debonair,
have put one on, and gracefully do you wear
that erudition of which it is the mark.

This is why our prince, valiant and wise,
chose you to serve as his ambassador
and represent him honorably before
the world that cannot help but recognize

those virtues he has trusted—as do I,
who've had the chance to follow your career
and watched as you served so well his interests here
in a court your presence could only dignify.

What's pleasant in my book, I offer you: clever,
scandalous here and there, but I trust, beguiling,
amusing, sometimes complaining, but mostly smiling.
With your approval I trust it may live forever.

» » » A Son Livre

Mon livre (et je ne suis sur ton aise envieux),
Tu t'en iras sans moi voir la Cour de mon Prince.
Hé, chétif que je suis, combien en gré je prinsse
Qu'un heur pareil au tien fût permis à mes yeux!

Là si quelqu'un vers toi se montre gracieux,
Souhaite-lui qu'il vive heureux en sa province:
Mais si quelque malin obliquement te pince,
Souhaite-lui tes pleurs et mon mal ennuyeux.

Souhaite-lui encor qu'il fasse un long voyage,
Et bien qu'il ait de vue éloigné son ménage,
Que son cœur, où qu'il voise, y soit toujours présent:

Souhaite qu'il vieillisse en longue servitude,
Qu'il n'éprouve à la fin que toute ingratitude,
Et qu'on mange son bien pendant qu'il est absent.

» » » To His Book

My book (and I'm not full of envy: I try not to be),
you're off to court without me, to see the prince,
while I languish behind and try hard not to wince.
If I could see for myself what your eyes will see!

If anyone there is polite to you or shows you
courtesy, wish him that he may live well and at home.
To the smart-ass who gives you grief, I'll send on some
of my many troubles. I think I can spare a few:

wish him a difficult voyage. May he go far
from home, where his heart is and his loved ones are,
while his hopes of returning one day grow ever more dim.

Pray that he may grow old in his servitude,
reaping the meager rewards of ingratitude
and learning at last how, at home, they've forgotten him.

Je ne veux point fouiller au sein de la nature,
Je ne veux point chercher l'esprit de l'univers,
Je ne veux point sonder les abîmes couverts,
Ni dessiner du ciel la belle architecture.

Je ne peins mes tableaux de si riche peinture,
Et si hauts arguments ne recherche à mes vers:
Mais suivant de ce lieu les accidents divers,
Soit de bien, soit de mal, j'écris à l'aventure.

Je me plains à mes vers, si j'ai quelque regret:
Je me ris avec eux, je leur dis mon secret,
Comme étant de mon cœur les plus sûrs secrétaires.

Aussi ne veux-je tant les peigner et friser,
Et de plus braves noms ne les veux déguiser
Que de papiers journaux ou bien de commentaires.

I don't want to pry into nature's secrets; I don't
question the plan of the universe. This is
hardly for me. To plumb the ocean's abysses
or the heavens' architecture? No, thank you, I won't.

Such big pictures in bright poster colors are not
my thing. To such lofty heights I do not aspire
in verse. My tastes are more modest; my wit is drier;
and for better or worse I work with what I've got.

I pick up my pen to doodle and scribble. I write
whatever crosses my mind and take delight
in candor—as if to a confidential clerk.

No rodomontade or circumlocutions of tact,
but simple statements of honest matters of fact,
like the memoranda a man might produce at work.

Un plus savant que moi, Paschal, ira songer
Avecques l'Ascréan dessus la double cime:
Et pour être de ceux dont on fait plus d'estime,
Dedans l'onde au cheval tout nu s'ira plonger.

Quant à moi, je ne veux, pour un vers allonger,
M'accourcir le cerveau: ni pour polir ma rime,
Me consumer l'esprit d'une soigneuse lime,
Frapper dessus ma table ou mes ongles ronger.

Aussi veux-je, Paschal, que ce que je compose
Soit une prose en rime ou une rime en prose,
Et ne veux pour cela le laurier mériter.

Et peut-être que tel se pense bien habile,
Qui trouvant de mes vers la rime si facile,
En vain travaillera, me voulant imiter.

Paschal, a smarter man than I am, would brood
with Hesiod upon that double peak
where, for the sake of his good repute, he'd seek
to skinny-dip in Pegasus's cold flood.

No rigors like that for me. I'd rather pad
the line a little, setting up for a rhyme,
or bite my nails, or drum my fingers in time
to the meter in hopes that I may improve what's bad

to something that would pass if it were prose.
I don't expect a laurel crown for those
exercises, Paschal. That's not what I'm after.

But let those who think it's so easy try it. They will
find that the task is beyond them, requiring skill
in the lack of which they'll provoke derisive laughter.

N'étant, comme je suis, encore exercité
Par tant et tant de maux au jeu de la fortune,
Je suivais d'Apollon la trace non commune,
D'une sainte fureur saintement agité.

Ores ne sentant plus cette divinité,
Mais piqué du souci qui fâcheux m'importune,
Une adresse j'ai pris beaucoup plus opportune
A qui se sent forcé de la nécessité.

Et c'est pourquoi, Seigneur, ayant perdu la trace
Que suit votre Ronsard par les champs de la Grâce,
Je m'adresse où je vois le chemin plus battu:

Ne me battant le cœur, la force, ni l'haleine,
De suivre, comme lui, par sueur et par peine,
Ce pénible sentier qui mène à la vertu.

I used to fret, beset by all my ills
that Fortune had dealt in a long series of bad
hands. I followed Apollo, or tried to, and had
that holy passion the god sometimes instills.

That's over and done. Those fires have burnt low,
and I'm prompted now by those troubles that evoke
a different set of responses. The cruel joke
is that they've taught me much of what I know.

Which is why, Seigneur, having failed in my ascent
to Ronsard's heights on Parnassus, I am content
with these modest trails in the foothills that I keep to.

I know my heart, my wind, my limitations.
To follow his splendid example? It's a temptation
to excellence I resist, as I've learned to do.

Je ne veux feuilleter les exemplaires Grecs,
Je ne veux retracer les beaux traits d'un Horace,
Et moins veux-je imiter d'un Pétrarque la grâce,
Ou la voix d'un Ronsard, pour chanter mes Regrets.

Ceux qui sont de Phœbus vrais poètes sacrés
Animeront leurs vers d'une plus grande audace:
Moi, qui suis agité d'une fureur plus basse,
Je n'entre si avant en si profonds secrets.

Je me contenterai de simplement écrire
Ce que la passion seulement me fait dire,
Sans rechercher ailleurs plus graves arguments.

Aussi n'ai-je entrepris d'imiter en ce livre
Ceux qui par leurs écrits se vantent de revivre
Et se tirer tout vifs dehors des monuments.

I won't riffle the pages of Greeks or try
to rework some elegant argument Horace made.
Still less do I want to stand in Petrarch's shade
or imitate Ronsard when the subject is my

own regrets. The Apollonians know
how to effect the grand gesture with ease
and style, but I confess I'm not one of these,
and for my peeves and private complaints a low

and more modest style is rather more apropos.
I scratch with my pen whatever may itch, and go
wherever my whims may lead. I follow my bent.

I mean this book to be true to life as we live it.
I will not falsify or try to give it
the grandeur of some pretentious monument.

Ceux qui sont amoureux, leurs amours chanteront,
Ceux qui aiment l'honneur, chanteront de la gloire,
Ceux qui sont près du roi, publieront sa victoire,
Ceux qui sont courtisans, leurs faveurs vanteront,

Ceux qui aiment les arts, les sciences diront,
Ceux qui sont vertueux, pour tels se feront croire,
Ceux qui aiment le vin, deviseront de boire,
Ceux qui sont de loisir, de fables écriront,

Ceux qui sont médisants, se plairont à médire,
Ceux qui sont moins fâcheux, diront des mots pour rire,
Ceux qui sont plus vaillants, vanteront leur valeur,

Ceux qui se plaisent trop, chanteront leur louange,
Ceux qui veulent flatter, feront d'un diable un ange:
Moi, qui suis malheureux, je plaindrai mon malheur.

Lovers will celebrate their beloveds, while those
who lust for glory and honor will tend to address
those grand subjects. For men near the king, the noblesse
and life at court will be what they'll expose.

Those into arts or the sciences will lecture;
those who believe in their virtue will get up and preach.
Connoisseurs of wines will enumerate for us each
cuvée's merits and faults, while the dreamers conjecture

what real life might be like. Bearers of tales
will gossip. And those whose bravery never fails
will rehearse their adventures. Jokers will joke with delight.

Egoists? They'll talk of themselves, and with passion,
and flatterers, flatter in ever more fulsome fashion.
And me? I'm depressed. I'll complain about my sad plight.

Las, où est maintenant ce mépris de fortune?
Où est ce cœur vainqueur de toute adversité,
Cet honnête désir de l'immortalité,
Et cette honnête flamme au peuple non commune?

Où sont ces doux plaisirs, qu'au soir sous la nuit brune
Les Muses me donnaient, alors qu'en liberté
Dessus le vert tapis d'un rivage écarté
Je les menais danser aux rayons de la lune?

Maintenant la fortune est maîtresse de moi,
Et mon cœur, qui soulait être maître de soi,
Est serf de mille maux et regrets qui m'ennuient,

De la postérité je n'ai plus de souci,
Cette divine ardeur, je ne l'ai plus aussi,
Et les Muses de moi, comme étranges, s'enfuient.

That contempt I had for Fortune, where has it gone?
Where is my brave heart that was proof against all
adversity's blows and ever alert to the call
of immortal fame? That talent not everyone

is given, I was blessed with, and late at night
the Muses would visit me. We used to frolic
on the grassy riverbanks of a bucolic
moonlit paradise in which I'd write.

Now Fortune is my mistress, rather sterner,
even severe; I am her slow learner;
and depression is the lesson plan of the day.

Posterity? That's forgotten. And the ardor
I used to have is gone, and writing is harder.
The Muses, strangers now, have fled away.

Cependant que la Cour mes ouvrages lisait,
Et que la sœur du roi, l'unique Marguerite,
Me faisant plus d'honneur que n'était mon mérite,
De son bel œil divin mes vers favorisait,

Une fureur d'esprit au ciel me conduisait
D'une aile qui la mort et les siècles évite,
Et le docte troupeau qui sur Parnasse habite,
De son feu plus divin mon ardeur attisait.

Ores je suis muet, comme on voit la Prophète,
Ne sentant plus le dieu qui la tenait sujette,
Perdre soudainement la fureur et la voix.

Et qui ne prend plaisir qu'un prince lui commande?
L'honneur nourrit les arts, et la Muse demande
Le théâtre du peuple et la faveur des rois.

Back when the court used to read what I would write,
and the king's sister Marguerite, that nonpareil,
would do me more honor than I deserved and say
such extravagant things, my spirit would take flight

to soar in the heavens on wings that time and death
could never touch, and the Muses, urging me higher,
would warm my ardor at their sacred fire.
That inspiration is gone now, and I draw breath

in the sorry silence of one whose holy seer
has lost that god to whom she once was dear
and who no longer will speak through her or sing.

Who is not flattered when a prince commands?
Honors nourish art, and the Muse demands
a public to perform for, and a king.

Ne t'ebahis, Ronsard, la moitié de mon âme,
Si de ton du Bellay France ne lit plus rien,
Et si avec l'air du ciel italien
Il n'a humé l'ardeur qui l'Italie enflamme.

Le saint rayon qui part des beaux yeux de ta dame
Et la sainte faveur de ton prince et du mien,
Cela, Ronsard, cela, cela mérite bien
De t'échauffer le cœur d'une si vive flamme.

Mais moi, qui suis absent des rais de mon soleil,
Comment puis-je sentir échauffement pareil
A celui qui est près de sa flamme divine?

Les coteaux soleillés de pampre sont couverts,
Mais des Hyperborées les éternels hivers
Ne portent que le froid, la neige et la bruine.

Ronsard, who are half of my soul, it is no surprise
that France these days is not reading du Bellay.
Italian smog, I'm afraid, gets in the way,
making it hard to see, and fills the skies.

In France, the sacred light that comes from the eyes
of one's beloved, or having the prince's ear . . .
That is a poet's perfect weather, my dear
Ronsard: it encourages him as he applies

his pen to paper! But here the skies are gray
with scudding clouds. That clear air far away
you flourish in I long for. I think of you so,

strolling among the flowers on sun-baked hills,
while here, where I find myself, a cold wind chills,
and drizzle comes down, and driving rain, and snow.

France, mère des arts, des armes et des lois,
Tu m'as nourri longtemps du lait de ta mamelle:
Ores, comme un agneau qui sa nourrice appelle,
Je remplis de ton nom les antres et les bois.

Si tu m'as pour enfant avoué quelquefois,
Que ne me réponds-tu maintenant, ô cruelle?
France, France, réponds à ma triste querelle.
Mais nul, sinon Écho, ne répond à ma voix.

Entre les loups cruels j'erre parmi la plaine,
Je sens venir l'hiver, de qui la froide haleine
D'une tremblante horreur fait hérisser ma peau.

Las, tes autres agneaux n'ont faute de pâture,
Ils ne craignent le loup, le vent ni la froidure:
Si ne suis-je pourtant le pire du troupeau.

O France, mother of arts, of arms, and of laws,
you used to give me your breasts' rich nourishment,
but now, a lost lamb, bleating his lament,
I call your name through the dark wood of my woes.

You acknowledged me once as your own son, but then
you became cruel and distant. Why was this?
O France, I deserve an answer, but all there is
is silence and its dismal echo when

among the ravening wolves I call to you.
Winter is coming with its cold breath, and through
my bones I feel it send a shiver of fear.

The other lambs of your flock are safe in the fold,
where they have no fear of wolves or of winter's cold . . .
And I know I am not the worst animal here.

Ce n'est le fleuve tusque au superbe rivage,
Ce n'est l'air des Latins, ni le mont Palatin,
Qui ores, mon Ronsard, me fait parler latin,
Changeant à l'étranger mon naturel langage.

C'est l'ennui de me voir trois ans et davantage,
Ainsi qu'un Prométhée, cloué sur l'Aventin,
Où l'espoir misérable et mon cruel destin,
Non le joug amoureux, me détient en servage.

Eh quoi, Ronsard, eh quoi, si au bord étranger
Ovide osa sa langue en barbare changer
Afin d'être entendu, qui me pourra reprendre

D'un change plus heureux? nul, puisque le français,
Quoiqu'au grec et romain égalé tu te sois,
Au rivage latin ne se peut faire entendre.

It isn't the proud banks of this Tuscan river
or the fine air of Rome, or the Palatine
that prompts me to Latin, Ronsard, O friend of mine,
instead of my native language for this palaver.

It's trouble you can blame, after these three long
years . . . A Prometheus fastened here to his rock
and tormented by hopes and the fates that mock
those hopes. You think they are bonds of love? You're wrong.

Ah, no, Ronsard, if Ovid's Latin could change
to barbarous Getic because no one in that strange
outpost could otherwise understand him, who

can blame me for this civilized shift? You speak
a French as polished as any Latin or Greek,
but here not a single thought or word would get through.

Bien qu'aux arts d'Apollon le vulgaire n'aspire,
Bien que de tels trésors l'avarice n'ait soin,
Bien que de tels harnais le soldat n'ait besoin,
Bien que l'ambition tels honneurs ne désire:

Bien que ce soit aux grands un argument de rire,
Bien que les plus rusés s'en tiennent le plus loin,
Et bien que du Bellay soit suffisant témoin
Combien est peu prisé le métier de la lyre:

Bien qu'un art sans profit ne plaise au courtisan,
Bien qu'on ne paye en vers l'œuvre d'un artisan,
Bien que la Muse soit de pauvreté suivie,

Si ne veux-je pourtant délaisser de chanter,
Puisque le seul chant peut mes ennuis enchanter,
Et qu'aux Muses je dois bien six ans de ma vie.

Apollo's art is not for the vulgar herd.
It's hardly a way for the greedy to make big money.
Ambitious men think of poetry as a funny
waste of their time. In a soldier's pack, it's absurd

to expect a book of verse. The bigwigs shun it.
The clever are clever enough to keep their distance.
It's a sorry business. Take du Bellay, for instance,
to demonstrate the scorn people heap upon it.

Courtiers think it is profitless and dumb.
Artisans want to be paid in advance—if they come.
The Muse is a bad mistress, a worse wife.

I remain, nonetheless, faithful. I will not quit.
It's only my writing that comforts me a bit,
And I thank the Muse for the last six years of my life.

Vu le soin ménager dont travaillé je suis,
Vu l'importun souci qui sans fin me tourmente,
Et vu tant de regrets desquels je me lamente,
Tu t'ébahis souvent comment chanter je puis.

Je ne chante, Magny, je pleure mes ennuis,
Ou, pour le dire mieux, en pleurant je les chante,
Si bien qu'en les chantant, souvent je les enchante:
Voilà pourquoi, Magny, je chante jours et nuits.

Ainsi chante l'ouvrier en faisant son ouvrage,
Ainsi le laboureur faisant son labourage,
Ainsi le pèlerin regrettant sa maison,

Ainsi l'aventurier en songeant à sa dame,
Ainsi le marinier en tirant à la rame,
Ainsi le prisonnier maudissant sa prison.

Consider the list of chores I've got, the small
details and many larger cares that burden
my soul, and consider too the flourishing garden
of my regrets . . . It's a wonder I write at all.

But I don't sing, Magny, except to complain.
You might say I've turned sobbing into singing,
an enchanting chanting I've learned in the hope of bringing
some relief to these days and nights of pain.

So does the craftsman sing as he works, and so
does the day laborer sing to himself although
he hates his task. And the plowman sings as well

out in the field. And the poor pilgrim who longs
for home will sing, and the lover has his songs,
and the galley slave, and the prisoner in his cell.

» 13

Maintenant je pardonne à la douce fureur
Qui m'a fait consumer le meilleur de mon âge,
Sans tirer autre fruit de mon ingrat ouvrage
Que le vain passe-temps d'une si longue erreur.

Maintenant je pardonne à ce plaisant labeur,
Puisque seul il endort le souci qui m'outrage,
Et puisque seul il fait qu'au milieu de l'orage,
Ainsi qu'auparavant, je ne tremble de peur.

Si les vers ont été l'abus de ma jeunesse,
Les vers seront aussi l'appui de ma vieillesse,
S'ils furent ma folie, ils seront ma raison,

S'ils furent ma blessure, ils seront mon Achille,
S'ils furent mon venin, le scorpion utile
Qui sera de mon mal la seule guérison.

Now I forgive that sweet insanity
that made me spend the best years of my age
in labor that never brought me any wage
but the passage of time in a way that was pleasing to me.

I think more kindly of all that expenditure
of effort through which was I able to find release
from my cares, or at least the hope that they might cease
testing me to see what I could endure.

If verse was my youthful folly, it has become
useful in my old age: what once was dumb
and crazy now seems sane and even smart.

What was my wound is now Achilles' healing;
what was the poison is antidote and appealing,
the cure I need, the balm for a troubled heart.

Si l'importunité d'un créditeur ma fâche,
Les vers m'ôtent l'ennui du fâcheux créditeur:
Et si je suis fâché d'un fâcheux serviteur,
Dessus les vers, Boucher, soudain je me défâche.

Si quelqu'un dessus moi sa colère délâche,
Sur les vers je vomis le venin de mon cœur:
Et si mon faible esprit est recru du labeur,
Les vers font que plus frais je retourne à ma tâche.

Les vers chassent de moi la molle oisiveté,
Les vers me font aimer la douce liberté,
Les vers chantent pour moi ce que dire je n'ose.

Si donc j'en recueillis tant de profits divers,
Demandes-tu, Boucher, de quoi servent les vers,
Et quel bien je reçois de ceux que je compose?

If my creditors' importunity is upsetting,
I can reverse my situation and am,
in verse, well off. Or if some cheeky, ham-
handed craftsman's botched work seems to be getting

me down, I can turn to well-made verse that soothes
my jangled nerves, Boucher, and find a sweet
repose in the ordered march of metric feet.
When I'm exhausted, its inexhaustible truths

drive away my fatigue and it restores
my spirits. The idle hour that otherwise bores,
I use. It is freedom itself at my beck and call.

It says those things I dare not on my own hook.
What earthly good does it do me, Boucher? Look!
Writing verse, I don't do badly at all.

Panjas, veux-tu savoir quels sont mes passe-temps?
Je songe au lendemain, j'ai soin de la dépense
Qui se fait chacun jour, et si faut que je pense
A rendre sans argent cent créditeurs contents.

Je vais, je viens, je cours, je ne perds point le temps,
Je courtise un banquier, je prends argent d'avance:
Quand j'ai dépêché l'un, un autre recommence,
Et ne fais pas le quart de ce que je prétends.

Qui me présente un compte, une lettre, un mémoire,
Qui me dit que demain est jour de consistoire,
Qui me rompt le cerveau de cent propos divers,

Qui se plaint, qui se deult, qui murmure, qui crie:
Avecques tout cela, dis, Panjas, je te prie,
Ne t'ébahis-tu point comment je fais des vers?

Panjas, you know how I pass my time these days?
I dream of tomorrow's bills or today's, past due,
and of all my hundreds of creditors, which few
I may have to pay with whatever I can raise

as I scurry here and there. I am always running
to borrow trifling sums from men of large means,
while I'm hounded by dogged men who are brandishing
    liens
and writs and all those armaments of dunning.

My desk is a heap of notices on loans
my friends have countersigned, and I hear moans
and threats and complaints all day long, and curses.

They're all of them quite justified, and I
agree with them, Panjas. And can you make out why
and how I can spend my time this way, writing verses?

Cependant que Magny suit son grand Avanson,
Panjas son cardinal, et moi le mien encore,
Et que l'espoir flatteur, qui nos beaux ans dévore,
Appâte nos désirs d'un friand hameçon.

Tu courtises les rois, et d'un plus heureux son
Chantant l'heur de Henri, qui son siècle décore,
Tu t'honores toi-même, et celui qui honore
L'honneur que tu lui fais par ta docte chanson.

Las, et nous cependant nous consumons notre âge
Sur le bord inconnu d'un étrange rivage,
Où le malheur nous fait ces tristes vers chanter:

Comme on voit quelquefois, quand la mort les appelle,
Arrangés flanc à flanc parmi l'herbe nouvelle,
Bien loin sur un étang trois cygnes lamenter.

Magny follows the seigneur d'Avanson,
and Panjas his Cardinal Armagnac, while I
work for my Cardinal du Bellay and try
to please him. Look at the three of us, each one

so attentive and eager. And you, Ronsard,
address kings, praising Henri, ornament
of the age, who repays with more than equivalent
honor, the honor you do him as his bard.

We, meanwhile, are spending our best years
on the banks of a strange river on which appears
this trio of forlorn, mortally stricken swans.

We complain about our luck as we graze on the grass
side by side, and time and the current pass,
and we long for that distant lake, our home, and France.

Après avoir longtemps erré sur le rivage
Où l'on voit lamenter tant de chétifs de cour,
Tu as atteint le bord où tout le monde court,
Fuyant de pauvreté le pénible servage.

Nous autres cependant, le long de cette plage,
En vain tendons les mains vers le nautonnier sourd,
Qui nous chasse bien loin: car, pour le faire court,
Nous n'avons un quatrain pour payer le naulage.

Ainsi donc tu jouis du repos bienheureux,
Et comme font là-bas ces doctes amoureux,
Bien avant dans un bois te perds avec ta dame:

Tu bois le long oubli de tes travaux passés,
Sans plus penser en ceux que tu as délaissés,
Criant dessus le port ou tirant à la rame.

After long wandering on this dismal shore
where so many poor mugs mill about and complain,
you've reached that further bank beyond all pain
and poverty which can trouble you no more.

The rest of us whom you've left behind stretch out
our empty hands, wanting the ferryman's penny
without which he will not give passage to any,
for charity is not what he is about.

Enjoy your life of ease and blessed leisure.
With your lady, wander the bosky groves of pleasure
there in that realm of culture and learning you've reached,

and drink oblivion's draft that will cleanse your mind
of thoughts of the past and of us whom you've left behind
suffering here at the jetty, crying, beached.

Si tu ne sais, Morel, ce que je fais ici,
Je ne fais pas l'amour ni autre tel ouvrage:
Je courtise mon maître, et si fais davantage,
Ayant de sa maison le principal souci.

Mon Dieu (ce diras-tu), quel miracle est-ce ci,
Que de voir Du Bellay se mêler du ménage
Et composer des vers en un autre langage?
Les loups et les agneaux s'accordent tout ainsi.

Voilà que c'est, Morel: la douce poésie
M'accompagne partout, sans qu'autre fantaisie
En si plaisant labeur me puisse rendre oisif.

Mais tu me répondras: Donne, si tu es sage,
De bonne heure congé au cheval qui est d'âge,
De peur qu'il ne s'empire et devienne poussif.

Morel, you have no idea how I'm living now.
Making love? Carousing? Nothing like that.
I serve my master, endlessly busy at
the management of household details. How

can such a thing have happened, you ask? Du Bellay
mixed up with such stuff? While writing Latin verse?
Wolves and sheep couldn't get along any worse.
But that's how it is, Morel. What can I say?

The poetry keeps me going, keeps me sane,
and allows me to escape for a moment the strain
of the job I do. Your answer comes to mind

at once: "You're trying to ride that warhorse still?
Get off. It's old! Put it out to pasture. It will
gallop no more, swaybacked and out of wind."

Cependant que tu dis ta Cassandre divine,
Les louanges du roi, et l'héritier d'Hector,
Et ce Montmorency, notre français Nestor,
Et que de sa faveur Henri t'estime digne:

Je me promène seul sur la rive latine,
La France regrettant, et regrettant encor
Mes antiques amis, mon plus riche trésor,
Et le plaisant séjour de ma terre angevine.

Je regrette les bois, et les champs blondissants,
Les vignes, les jardins, et les prés verdissants
Que mon fleuve traverse: ici pour récompense

Ne voyant que l'orgueil de ces monceaux pierreux,
Où me tient attaché d'un espoir malheureux
Ce que possède moins celui qui plus y pense.

You praise Cassandra as divine; you praise
the king, whom you describe as the heir of Hector;
in our Montmorency you see a Nestor;
and Henri shows you favor in all ways.

I walk alone on the banks of the Tiber in Rome,
regretting France, regretting the loss of all
those dear old friends whose faces I recall
as vividly as the look of my Anjou home

with its woods and wheat fields I so sorely miss
and vineyards, gardens, and meadows—and through all this
another river runs. At my present address,

heaps of gray stones are piled high in pride to loom
and blot out light and hope, and I walk in their gloom
that more and more I admire less and less.

Heureux, de qui la mort de sa gloire est suivie,
Et plus heureux celui dont l'immortalité
Ne prend commencement de la postérité,
Mais devant que la mort ait son âme ravie.

Tu jouis, mon Ronsard, même durant ta vie,
De l'immortel honneur que tu as mérité:
Et devant que mourir (rare félicité)
Ton heureuse vertu triomphe de l'envie.

Courage donc, Ronsard, la victoire est à toi,
Puisque de ton côté est la faveur du roi:
Jà du laurier vainqueur tes tempes se couronnent,

Et jà la tourbe épaisse à l'entour de ton flanc
Ressemble ces esprits, qui là-bas environnent
Le grand prêtre de Thrace au long sourpelis blanc.

Happy is he at whose death glory starts,
but even happier he who need not wait
for posterity to declare that he was great
and is so recognized before he departs.

You, my Ronsard, while still alive know such
honor and it is surely merited.
Your virtues everywhere are credited,
and accomplishments that not even envy can touch.

Courage, Ronsard, the victory is won.
The king speaks well of you to everyone.
You wear, while here, that laurel to which we aspire.

Admirers crowd around as you make your way,
as the spirits of the underworld did, they say,
when Orpheus passed by them, strumming his lyre.

Comte, qui ne fis onc compte de la grandeur,
Ton Du Bellay n'est plus: ce n'est plus qu'une souche,
Qui dessus un ruisseau d'un dos courbé se couche,
Et n'a plus rien de vif, qu'un petit de verdeur.

Si j'écris quelquefois, je n'écris point d'ardeur,
J'écris naïvement tout ce qu'au cœur me touche,
Soit de bien, soit de mal, comme il vient à la bouche,
En un style aussi lent que lente est ma froideur.

Vous autres cependant, peintres de la nature,
Dont l'art n'est pas enclos dans une portraiture,
Contrefaites des vieux les ouvrages plus beaux.

Quant à moi, je n'aspire à si haute louange,
Et ne sont mes portraits auprès de vos tableaux
Non plus qu'est un Janet auprès d'un Michel-Ange.

Count, who never took much account of grandeur,
your du Bellay has had it, a torn-up stump
that straddles the stream, its roots in the air, its damp
bark emitting shoots of hopeless verdure.

If I still write, sometimes, it is not with ardor,
but only to set down whatever crosses my mind
in whatever language that I am able to find,
graceless and slow, and even that grows harder.

You others out there trying to paint from nature,
taking pains to execute each feature
precisely, you are beyond me: I have no

such aspirations. These quick sketches are
the best I can do, inferior by far—
a Janet across from a Michelangelo.

Ores, plus que jamais, me plaît d'aimer la Muse
Soit qu'en français j'écrive ou langage romain,
Puisque le jugement d'un prince tant humain
De si grande faveur envers les lettres use.

Donc le sacré métier où ton esprit s'amuse
Ne sera désormais un exercice vain,
Et le tardif labeur que nous promet ta main
Désormais pour Francus n'aura plus nulle excuse.

Cependant, mon Ronsard, pour tromper mes ennuis,
Et non pour m'enrichir, je suivrai, si je puis,
Les plus humbles chansons de ta Muse lassée.

Ainsi chacun n'a pas mérité que d'un roi
La libéralité lui fasse, comme à toi,
Ou son archet doré, ou sa lyre crossée.

Now, more than ever, I must love the Muse,
whether I write in my native French or choose
Latin. The approbation of a great
and enlightened prince who can appreciate

literature is what all of us desire.
He encourages us and makes us all aim higher.
Your *Franciade*, Ronsard, is overdue,
and you apply yourself, as I must, too,

to console myself here, even though I have no
hope of riches or those flights you do so
impressively well. Yet may I aspire

to an excellence like yours that well deserves
the rewards from that wise and liberal king it serves—
a golden bow and a crozier-headed lyre.

Ne lira-t-on jamais que ce dieu rigoureux?
Jamais ne lira-t-on que cette Idalienne?
Ne verra-t-on jamais Mars sans la Cyprienne?
Jamais ne verra-t-on que Ronsard amoureux?

Retistra-t-on toujours, d'un tour laborieux,
Cette toile, argument d'une si longue peine?
Reverra-t-on toujours Oreste sur la scène?
Sera toujours Roland par amour furieux?

Ton Francus, cependant, a beau hausser les voiles,
Dresser le gouvernail, épier les étoiles,
Pour aller où il dût être ancré désormais:

Il a le vent à gré, il est en équipage,
Il est encor pourtant sur le troyen rivage,
Aussi crois-je, Ronsard, qu'il n'en partit jamais.

Why do we have to read all the time of love
and Cupid, that pest on Ida's treacherous heights?
Why must Mars have Venus to trouble his nights?
Ronsard, is that what we all must be writing of

incessantly, the same routine, the same
story—whether Orestes or Roland performs
in close-order drill that manual of arms?
Must Francus in your epic play that game?

He holds the tiller and looks up into the sky
to plot his course by the stars, and he's standing by,
eager, awaiting a fresh fair wind, while we

wish him Godspeed. But he's stuck there on the sands
of Troy with his ship and crew. Summon all hands
and let him, my dear Ronsard, put out to sea.

Qu'heureux tu es, Baïf, heureux, et plus qu'heureux,
De ne suivre abusé cette aveugle déesse,
Qui d'un tour inconstant et nous hausse et nous baisse,
Mais cet aveugle enfant qui nous fait amoureux!

Tu n'éprouves, Baïf, d'un maître rigoureux
Le sévère sourcil: mais la douce rudesse
D'une belle, courtoise et gentille maîtresse,
Qui fait languir ton cœur doucement langoureux.

Moi chétif, cependant, loin des yeux de mon prince,
Je vieillis malheureux en étrange province,
Fuyant la pauvreté: mais las ne fuyant pas

Les regrets, les ennuis, le travail et la peine,
Le tardif repentir d'une espérance vaine,
Et l'importun souci, qui me suit pas à pas.

How fortunate you are, Baïf, twice, thrice
fortunate, not to be in the thrall of the blind
goddess who keeps us hoping but then is unkind,
as the boy is too, whose torments are not nice.

You do not feel a master's rigor or know
his scowl, Baïf, but encounter the gentler look
of a sweet and lovely lady who can crook
her finger in a summons sweet and slow.

I, meanwhile, so far from my prince's eyes,
am growing old beneath unfamiliar skies
and flagging as I run a losing race

with poverty, while exasperation, pain,
and absurd regret are keeping up. In vain
I exert myself, for they set a demanding pace.

Malheureux l'an, le mois, le jour, l'heure et le point,
Et malheureuse soit la flatteuse espérance,
Quand pour venir ici j'abandonnai la France:
La France, et mon Anjou, dont le désir me point.

Vraiment d'un bon oiseau guidé je ne fus point,
Et mon cœur me donnait assez signifiance
Que le ciel était plein de mauvaise influence,
Et que Mars était lors à Saturne conjoint.

Cent fois le bon avis lors m'en voulut distraire,
Mais toujours le destin me tirait au contraire:
Et si mon désir n'eût aveuglé ma raison,

N'était-ce pas assez pour rompre mon voyage,
Quand sur le seuil de l'huis, d'un sinistre présage,
Je me blessai le pied sortant de ma maison?

Unlucky the year, the month, day, hour, and minute
and also the flattering hope that sent me here
to abandon the France I love and to leave that dear
Anjou that I long for now and my happiness in it.

A little birdie prompted me, an omen
most unpropitious that I distrusted because
the stars in the sky were wrong and red Mars was
conjoined with Saturn to promise good luck to no man.

A hundred times I hesitated, but still
fate pulled at my sleeve and bent my will,
desire blinding my reason. Filled with doubt,

I should have held back. And at my very door,
I stumbled and twisted an ankle, which is as poor
a way as I know for a poor fool to set out.

Si celui qui s'apprête à faire un long voyage
Doit croire celui-là qui a jà voyagé,
Et qui des flots marins longuement outragé,
Tout moite et dégouttant s'est sauvé du naufrage,

Tu me croiras, Ronsard, bien que tu sois plus sage,
Et quelque peu encor (ce crois-je) plus âgé,
Puisque j'ai devant toi en cette mer nagé,
Et que déjà ma nef découvre le rivage.

Donques je t'avertis que cette mer romaine,
De dangereux écueils et de bancs toute pleine,
Cache mille périls, et qu'ici bien souvent,

Trompé du chant pipeur des monstres de Sicile,
Pour Charybde éviter tu tomberas en Scylle,
Si tu ne sais nager d'une voile à tout vent.

If you're planning a trip, you ought to listen well
to someone who has already gone that way
and suffered the bumps in that road or felt the cold spray
of that rough passage and come back alive to tell

what he has seen. Listen, Ronsard, you are wiser
and older, I do believe, by a year or two,
but I have been there, and what I am telling you
of the seas of Rome is that they do run high, sir,

with their treacherous sandbars and shifting shoals
beneath the surface to ruin those trusting souls
who dared set forth, and there are the Sirens, too,

who beckon wickedly. You try to steer clear
of Charybdis only to find that Scylla is near,
and suddenly you're in the drink, and what can you do?

Ce n'est l'ambition, ni le soin d'acquérir,
Qui m'a fait délaisser ma rive paternelle,
Pour voir ces monts couverts d'une neige éternelle,
Et par mille dangers ma fortune quérir.

Le vrai honneur, qui n'est coutumier de périr,
Et la vraye vertu, qui seule est immortelle,
Ont comblé mes désirs d'une abondance telle,
Qu'un plus grand bien aux dieux je ne veux requérir.

L'honnête servitude où mon devoir me lie
M'a fait passer les monts de France en Italie,
Et demeurer trois ans sur ce bord étranger,

Où je vis languissant: ce seul devoir encore
Me peut faire changer France à l'Inde et au More,
Et le ciel à l'enfer me peut faire changer.

It wasn't ambition and surely not greed that sent
me out of my native valley to climb the Alpine
passes with their eternal snows. My design
wasn't to risk such dangers. I never meant

to gain for myself more honor than we get
from modest virtue's steady exercise.
(One finds that even a little satisfies
the appetite that innocent youth can whet.)

No, it was something else, my extravagant sense
of duty, that drove me across those mountains from
    France
to Italy, where I've been now three years in which

I've languished. And that same sense of duty could
have sent me from France to the ends of the earth for
    good,
or from heaven itself to hell—and I'd make the switch.

Quand je te dis adieu, pour m'en venir ici,
Tu me dis, mon La Haye, il m'en souvient encore:
Souvienne-toi, Bellay, de ce que tu es ore,
Et comme tu t'en vas, retourne-t'en ainsi.

Et tel comme je vins, je m'en retourne aussi:
Hormis un repentir qui le cœur me dévore,
Qui me ride le front, qui mon chef décolore,
Et qui me fait plus bas enfoncer le sourcil.

Ce triste repentir, qui me ronge et me lime,
Ne vient (car j'en suis net) pour sentir quelque crime,
Mais pour m'être trois ans à ce bord arrêté:

Et pour m'être abusé d'une ingrate espérance,
Qui pour venir ici trouver la pauvreté,
M'a fait (sot que je suis) abandonner la France.

When we bade one another adieu so that I could come
here, you said, Lahaye, I remember it clear
as yesterday: "Stay as you are. Don't change. You hear?
Be just the same when you come back, old chum."

And I am returning very nearly the same,
except for one regret that eats at my heart,
wrinkles my brow, has made my brown hair start
turning gray, and occasions frowns of shame.

The regret that gnaws at my vitals all the time
is not for having committed any crime
but only for those three years I've stayed away,

for kidding myself, for being such a dope
living always in poverty here and hope.
For this I abandoned France? What can I say?

Je hais plus que la mort un jeune casanier,
Qui ne sort jamais hors, sinon aux jours de fête,
Et craignant plus le jour qu'une sauvage bête,
Se fait en sa maison lui-même prisonnier.

Mais je ne puis aimer un vieillard voyager,
Qui court deçà delà, et jamais ne s'arrête,
Ains des pieds moins léger que léger de la tête,
Ne séjourne jamais non plus qu'un messager.

L'un sans se travailler en sûreté demeure,
L'autre, qui n'a repos jusques à tant qu'il meure,
Traverse nuit et jour mille lieux dangereux:

L'un passe riche et sot heureusement sa vie,
L'autre, plus souffreteux qu'un pauvre qui mendie,
S'acquiert en voyageant un savoir malheureux.

I hate more than death itself a stay-at-home,
a kid who never goes out except to a fete
and keeps in his house, afraid, in a cold sweat,
like a beast locked in a cage or an inmate in some

cell. But an old geezer who runs here and there,
with feet that skitter the way his mind does too,
always on his way, like the courier who
has an urgent dispatch to deliver to someone somewhere,

I also hate. And both of them are wrong:
the one who can't go and the one who can't stop for long.
The first is a coward, the other's a reckless crazy.

Both of them are wasting their lives, for they spend
their time as if they never believed it could end.
To know one's place in the world is not so easy.

Quiconque, mon Bailleul, fait longuement séjour
Sous un ciel inconnu, et quiconques endure
D'aller de port en port cherchant son aventure,
Et peut vivre étranger dessous un autre jour:

Qui peut mettre en oubli de ses parents l'amour,
L'amour de sa maîtresse, et l'amour que nature
Nous fait porter au lieu de notre nourriture,
Et voyage toujours sans penser au retour:

Il est fils d'un rocher ou d'une ourse cruelle,
Et digne qui jadis ait sucé la mamelle
D'une tigre inhumaine: encor ne voit-on point

Que les fiers animaux en leurs forts ne retournent,
Et ceux qui parmi nous domestiques séjournent,
Toujours de la maison le doux désir les point.

Whoever makes long journeys, Bailleul, under
unknown skies, whoever is able to stand
those embarkations from port to port in a grand
and endless search for adventure . . . Well, I wonder

how he can put his beloved parents out
of his mind, or his love of a girl. It's almost as weird
as a man's forgetting the place where he was reared.
These are the things I'm constantly dreaming about.

A person like that is the son of a stone and has
a heart of stone. He's wild as a bear cub or was
suckled by some tigress. But no, I'm unfair

to the feral creatures, which, as I realize,
show more refinement of feeling. An animal tries
after his hunt for food to slink back to his lair.

Heureux qui, comme Ulysse, a fait un beau voyage,
Ou comme celui-là qui conquit la toison,
Et puis est retourné, plein d'usage et raison,
Vivre entre ses parents le reste do son âge!

Quand reverrai-je, hélas, de mon petit village
Fumer la cheminée, et en quelle saison
Reverrai-je le clos de ma pauvre maison,
Qui m'est une province, et beaucoup davantage?

Plus me plaît le séjour qu'ont bâti mes aïeux
Que des palais romains le front audacieux,
Plus que le marbre dur me plaît l'ardoise fine,

Plus mon Loire gaulois que le Tibre latin,
Plus mon petit Liré que le mont Palatin,
Et plus que l'air marin la douceur angevine.

Happy is he who like Ulysses can reach
home, or like Jason, bearing his gold sheepskin,
can return, full of hard-earned wisdom, to live in
the admiration of those who remained on the beach.

Alas, when shall I see my village once more
with smoke curling up from its chimneys into a sky
familiar to me? At what time of the year will I
behold that house my ancestors built for

our comfort, more pleasing to me than any Roman
palaces? All this marble impresses no man
more than our simple honest slate. The Loire

I much prefer to the Tiber; the Liré of mine
is a handsomer hill I think than the Palatine;
and Anjou's air is better than Rome's by far.

Je me ferai savant en la philosophie,
En la mathématique et médecine aussi:
Je me ferai légiste, et d'un plus haut souci
Apprendrai les secrets de la théologie:

Du luth et du pinceau j'ébatterai ma vie,
De l'escrime et du bal. Je discourais ainsi,
Et me vantais en moi d'apprendre tout ceci,
Quand je changeai la France au séjour d'Italie.

O beaux discours humains! Je suis venu si loin,
Pour m'enrichir d'ennui, de vieillesse et de soin,
Et perdre en voyageant le meilleur de mon âge.

Ainsi le marinier souvent pour tout trésor
Rapporte des harengs en lieu de lingots d'or,
Ayant fait, comme moi, un malheureux voyage.

I will study ethics, logic, philosophy,
will teach myself mathematics, and medicine, too,
and jurisprudence—why not?—or I could do
something yet more demanding—theology!

And to pass the time, the charms of the easel and lute.
And fencing, of course, and dancing. That's what I'd say
I'd learn when I came from France for a brief stay
in Rome where learning would be my incessant pursuit.

So much for good intentions. Talk isn't hard.
My attainments are wrinkles and gray hairs, and I'm bored
and ashamed of myself for my waste of time. The wish

that prompts the sailor to set out may be for gold,
but what he brings back won't be treasure down in the hold
but only a worthless cargo of rotten fish.

Que ferai-je, Morel? Dis-moi, si tu l'entends,
Ferai-je encore ici plus longue demeurance,
Ou si j'irai revoir les campagnes de France,
Quand les neiges fondront au soleil du printemps?

Si je demeure ici, hélas, je perds mon temps
A me repaître en vain d'une longue espérance:
Et si je veux ailleurs fonder mon assurance,
Je fraude mon labeur du loyer que j'attends.

Mais faut-il vivre ainsi d'une espérance vaine?
Mais faut-il perdre ainsi bien trois ans de ma peine?
Je ne bougerai donc. Non, non, je m'en irai.

Je demourrai pourtant, si tu le me conseilles.
Hélas, mon cher Morel, dis-moi que je ferai,
Car je tiens, comme on dit, le loup par les oreilles.

What should I do, Morel? What would you propose?
Stay on here in this godforsaken city,
or return to France to see once again its pretty
countryside when the springtime is melting its snows?

If I remain here in Rome, I shall look like a fool,
hoping against hope that my life will improve,
but it all will have been for nothing if I now move,
give up, and go home an utter failure who'll

have totally wasted three years of his life. What would you
suggest: stick it out, or fold it in? I'll do
whatever you tell me. Which of these plans appears

slightly less stupid? I'm in a bad way
and sooner or later must fight or run. As they say
in the old proverb, I am holding the wolf by its ears.

Comme le marinier, que le cruel orage
A longtemps agité dessus la haute mer,
Ayant finalement à force de ramer
Garanti son vaisseau du danger du naufrage,

Regarde sur le port, sans plus craindre la rage
Des vagues ni des vents, les ondes écumer:
Et quelqu'autre bien loin, au danger d'abîmer,
En vain tendre les mains vers le front du rivage:

Ainsi, mon cher Morel, sur le port arrêté,
Tu regardes la mer, et vois en sûreté
De mille tourbillons son onde renversée:

Tu la vois jusqu'au ciel s'élever bien souvent,
Et vois ton du Bellay à la merci du vent
Assis au gouvernail dans une nef percée.

Like a sailor who knows too well what a storm can do,
having been battered and pitched by the high seas' fury
that can toss a huge vessel about like a dory,
and who thought that drowning was certain then but who

on the mole in the harbor later can watch, unafraid,
waves that whip the winds into sheets of spray
because it is someone else in peril today
who reaches up his hands and waves for aid:

so you, my dear Morel, stand there in the port,
observing the ocean's rage as if it were sport
when the breakers crash and whirlpools and eddies suck

flotsam down or fling it up in the air,
and you see your old friend, du Bellay, in despair,
in terror, clutching the tiller and out of luck.

La nef qui longuement a voyagé, Dillier,
Dedans le sein du port à la fin on la serre:
Et le bœuf, qui longtemps a renversé la terre,
Le bouvier à la fin lui ôte le collier:

Le vieux cheval se voit à la fin délier,
Pour ne perdre l'haleine ou quelque honte acquerre:
Et pour se reposer du travail de la guerre,
Se retire à la fin le vieillard chevalier:

Mais moi, qui jusqu'ici n'ai prouvé que la peine,
La peine et le malheur d'une espérance vaine,
La douleur, le souci, les regrets, les ennuis,

Je vieillis peu à peu sur l'onde ausonienne,
Et si n'espère point, quelque bien qui m'advienne,
De sortir jamais hors des travaux où je suis.

After its many voyages, Dillier,
the ship comes home to be drawn up on the shore,
and the ox that for years has plowed its furrows for
the farmer is unyoked at last in the way

the tired old horse is put out to pasture to graze
before its wind is broken and its back.
So does the cavalryman hang up his tack,
put war behind him, and have a few peaceful days.

But I, who all this time have known nothing but pain,
ill luck, frustration, regrets, and hopes that proved vain,
have grown old, little by little, here by the river

Tiber and cannot hope anymore for good
to knock on my door—and if it did I would
turn it away as a joke more cruel than clever.

Depuis que j'ai laissé mon naturel séjour
Pour venir où le Tibre aux flots tortus ondoie,
Le ciel a vu trois fois par son oblique voie
Recommencer son cours la grand lampe du jour.

Mais j'ai si grand désir de me voir de retour
Que ces trois ans me sont plus qu'un siège de Troie,
Tant me tarde, Morel, que Paris je revoie,
Et tant le ciel pour moi fait lentement son tour.

Il fait son tour si lent, et me semble si morne,
Si morne et si pesant, que le froid Capricorne
Ne m'accourcit les jours, ni le Cancre les nuits.

Voilà, mon cher Morel, combien le temps me dure
Loin de France et de toi, et comment la nature
Fait toute chose longue avecques mes ennuis.

Since I set out from my natural habitat
to come here to the tortuous Tiber, the sun
has moved three times to its extremes and run
its course now through twelve seasons. I reckon that

as long as the siege of Troy . . . It certainly feels
as long, and my desire to see again
the Paris that I have loved and the river Seine
is such that clocks appear to have stopped their wheels

and cogs, and time moves slowly, slowly, as if
it were worn down with my cares, and as stiff,
and Capricorn's cold days seem long, and the nights

of summer Cancer contrive somehow to extend
and torment me, Morel, so that they never end,
and nature draws everything out but my delights.

C'était ores, c'était qu'à moi je devais vivre,
Sans vouloir être plus que cela que je suis,
Et qu'heureux je devais de ce peu que je puis
Vivre content du bien de la plume et du livre.

Mais il n'a plu aux dieux me permettre de suivre
Ma jeune liberté, ni faire que depuis
Je vécusse aussi franc de travaux et d'ennuis,
Comme d'ambition j'étais franc et délivre.

Il ne leur a pas plu qu'en ma vieille saison
Je susse quel bien c'est de vivre en sa maison,
De vivre entre les siens sans crainte et sans envie:

Il leur a plu (hélas) qu'à ce bord étranger
Je visse ma franchise en prison se changer,
Et la fleur de mes ans en l'hiver de ma vie.

I remember how it used to be when I
was obliged to do no more than live and enjoy
what the family always had. As a little boy,
I was content with my pens and books, but my

liberty and my ease offended the great
gods, who never like to issue a pass
from work and worry. Not even ambition was
an excuse I could make for my discontent with my fate.

At the whim of cruel gods, a decree came down
that I should roam and live in some foreign town
and rather than sit in my own house be confined

in somebody else's servant quarters where
I feel too soon the chill of the winter air
and realize that my best years are behind.

» 38

O qu'heureux est celui qui peut passer son âge
Entre pareils à soi! et qui sans fiction,
Sans crainte, sans envie et sans ambition,
Règne paisiblement en son pauvre ménage!

Le misérable soin d'acquérir davantage
Ne tyrannise point sa libre affection,
Et son plus grand désir, désir sans passion,
Ne s'étend plus avant que son propre héritage.

Il ne s'empêche point des affaires d'autrui,
Son principal espoir ne dépend que de lui,
Il est sa cour, son roi, sa faveur et son maître.

Il ne mange son bien en pays étranger,
Il ne met pour autrui sa personne en danger,
Et plus riche qu'il est ne voudrait jamais être.

Happy is he who can spend his life with his own
kind, and who without any need for pretense,
and without ambition or envy, has the good sense
to live by the fireside he has always known,

untroubled by ambition's goad that distracts
from what his father and forebears always had
and were content with. He disdains the mad
passions of the madding crowd and the acts

of desperate men who scurry about in the street.
He is able to recognize what he has as sweet,
and enjoy being the master in his own hall.

He does not risk what he has for the sake of applause
or even his life itself in some foreign cause.
To be richer? That doesn't matter to him at all.

J'aime la liberté, et languis en service,
Je n'aime point la cour, et me faut courtiser,
Je n'aime la feintise, et me faut déguiser,
J'aime simplicité, et n'apprends que malice:

Je n'adore les biens, et sers à l'avarice,
Je n'aime les honneurs, et me les faut priser,
Je veux garder ma foi, et me la faut briser,
Je cherche la vertu, et ne trouve que vice:

Je cherche le repos, et trouver ne le puis,
J'embrasse le plaisir, et n'éprouve qu'ennuis,
Je n'aime à discourir, en raison je me fonde:

J'ai le corps maladif, et me faut voyager,
Je suis né pour la Muse, on me fait ménager:
Ne suis-je pas, Morel, le plus chétif du monde?

Liberty I love but I languish, waiting
on masters. The ways of the court where they scrape and
        bow
I've been forced to learn. And wretched pretense now
is almost second nature, despite my hating

all that I do and say. I was honest and candid
and disdained honors that now I chase after. And lies
I hear and I tell every day, although I despise
lying. I used to believe what a decent man did

was all that mattered, but I am surrounded by vice.
The peace that I loved is only in paradise.
I dream of pleasure and ease but each day is worse.

Disputes I hate but I argue, wrongly and badly.
Poetry was my passion, but lately, sadly,
I never have time. Morel, my life is a curse.

Un peu de mer tenait le grand Dulichien
D'Itaque séparé, l'Apennin porte-nue
Et les monts de Savoie à la tête chenue
Me tiennent loin de France au bord ausonien.

Fertile est mon séjour, stérile était le sien,
Je ne suis des plus fins, sa finesse est connue:
Les siens gardant son bien attendaient sa venue,
Mais nul en m'attendant ne me garde le mien.

Pallas sa guide était, je vais à l'aventure,
Il fut dur au travail, moi tendre de nature:
A la fin il ancra son navire à son port,

Je ne suis assuré de retourner en France:
Il fit de ses haineux une belle vengeance,
Pour me venger des miens je ne suis assez fort.

Only a little stretch of open sea
lay between Ulysses and his goal,
his home in Ithaca, but I have the whole
mass of the Apennines to separate me

in Italy from France, and I languish here.
The home I miss is rich, while his was poor
and mean. And I don't have his cleverness or
a son at home who waits for me to appear.

Great Pallas was his guide; I reckon blind.
He was strong and steady in his mind,
while I am flighty. He came to port at length.

I lack his faith in himself, his determination,
and am faint-hearted and wilt at intimidation,
and my enemies laugh at my evident lack of strength.

N'étant de mes ennuis la fortune assouvie,
Afin que je devinsse à moi-même odieux,
M'ôta de mes amis celui que j'aimais mieux,
Et sans qui je n'avais de vivre nulle envie.

Donc l'éternelle nuit a ta clarté ravie,
Et je ne t'ai suivi parmi ces obscurs lieux!
Toi, qui m'as plus aimé que ta vie et tes yeux,
Toi, que j'ai plus aimé que mes yeux et ma vie.

Hélas, cher compagnon, que ne puis-je être encor
Le frère de Pollux, toi celui de Castor,
Puisque notre amitié fut plus que fraternelle?

Reçois donques ces pleurs, pour gage de ma foi,
Et ces vers qui rendront, si je ne me deçoi,
De si rare amitié la mémoire éternelle.

Fortune thought my life too little troubled—
that I hadn't been well enough schooled in how to hate
it and myself—so it took away my great
friend whom I loved, and now my woes are doubled.

That light of my life is darkened now that you've gone,
and I'd follow you to the land of shades if I could.
You thought of my welfare more than of your own good,
as I cared more for your happiness than my own.

Alas, my dear companion, I can no more
be Pollux to your Castor as we were before,
for we were more than brothers, you and I.

Accept these tears I shed, the pledge of my faith.
Accept these verses I send now to your wraith,
recalling our friendship which can never die.

42

C'est ores, mon Vineus, mon cher Vineus, c'est ore,
Que de tous les chétifs le plus chétif je suis,
Et que ce que j'étais, plus être je ne puis,
Ayant perdu mon temps, et ma jeunesse encore.

La pauvreté me suit, le souci me dévore,
Tristes me sont les jours, et plus tristes les nuits.
O que je suis comblé de regrets et d'ennuis!
Plût à Dieu que je fusse un Pasquin ou Marphore,

Je n'aurais sentiment du malheur qui me point:
Ma plume serait libre et si ne craindrais point
Qu'un plus grand contre moi pût exercer son ire.

Assure-toi, Vineus, que celui seul est roi
A qui même les rois ne peuvent donner loi,
Et qui peut d'un chacun à son plaisir écrire.

» 42

Take a look at me, Vineus: what do you see?
Can you find any sadder sack? Of all the sons
of bitches you know, who is worse off? What I once
was I am no longer. A shadow of me

grows poorer and weaker and less, as care devours
my not-quite-dead-yet carcass. My days are wracked
with pain, but then at night I'd take them back
to flee my terrible dreams of the small hours.

If I had the gift for satire, I could express
my rage, my chagrin, and the envy I confess
that gnaws at me when I think about my betters.

But the man I envy most, old friend, is he
who never needs to be careful and feels free
to please only himself in the world of letters.

The Regrets 99

43

Je ne commis jamais fraude ni maléfice,
Je ne doutai jamais des points de notre foi,
Je n'ai point violé l'ordonnance du roi,
Et n'ai point éprouvé la rigueur de justice:

J'ai fait à mon seigneur fidèlement service,
Je fais pour mes amis ce que je puis et doy,
Et crois que jusqu'ici nul ne se plaint de moi,
Que vers lui j'aye fait quelque mauvais office.

Voilà ce que je suis. Et toutefois, Vineus,
Comme un qui est aux dieux et aux hommes haineux
Le malheur me poursuit et toujours m'importune:

Mais j'ai ce beau confort en mon adversité,
C'est qu'on dit que je n'ai ce malheur mérité,
Et que digne je suis de meilleure fortune.

» 43

I'm not a swindler, not a felon or thief;
I've never doubted the church's teachings, never
broken the king's ordinances or ever
been arrested or fined. To my belief,

I've served my master faithfully and been true,
and I've always helped my friends as much as was fair
and ethical. And nobody, anywhere,
can say I've done him wrong. But what good does it do?

I might as well have been a perfect swine,
a bad hat, Vineus, vicious and malign,
and my misery could not have been more severe.

I take what comfort I can when people say
it's outrageous that I'm punished in this way
and that I've deserved better is perfectly clear.

Si pour avoir passé sans crime sa jeunesse,
Si pour n'avoir d'usure enrichi sa maison,
Si pour n'avoir commis homicide ou traïson,
Si pour n'avoir usé de mauvaise finesse,

Si pour n'avoir jamais violé sa promesse,
On se doit réjouir en l'arrière-saison,
Je dois à l'avenir, si j'ai quelque raison,
D'un grand contentement consoler ma vieillesse.

Je me console donc en mon adversité,
Ne requérant aux dieux plus grand félicité
Que de pouvoir durer en cette patience.

O dieux, si vous avez quelque souci de nous,
Octroyez-moi ce don, que j'espère de vous,
Et pour votre pitié et pour mon innocence.

Having passed one's youth without having violated
the laws, without having cheated anyone
by making usurious loans, without having done
murder, without having ever prevaricated

or broken his promises, one then ought to find
happiness in the fullness of his years—
provided that he survives, still sees and hears,
and manages to retain his powers of mind.

With my bright prospects, I should be fine at length
and during my present adversities draw strength
from the thought. I need not pray to the gods for peace.

All I might want, if they felt disposed to bestow
a gift, would be that patience I now need so
badly. And pity. And hope that my troubles may cease.

O marâtre nature (et marâtre es-tu bien,
De ne m'avoir plus sage ou plus heureux fait naître),
Pourquoi ne m'as-tu fait de moi-même le maître,
Pour suivre ma raison et vivre du tout mien?

Je vois les deux chemins, et ce mal, et de bien:
Je sais que la vertu m'appelle à la main dextre,
Et toutefois il faut que je tourne à senestre,
Pour suivre un traître espoir, qui m'a fait du tout sien.

Et quel profit en ai-je? O belle récompense!
Je me suis consumé d'une vaine dépense,
Et n'ai fait autre acquêt que de mal et d'ennui.

L'étranger recueillit le fruit de mon service,
Je travaille mon corps d'un indigne exercice,
Et porte sur mon front la vergogne d'autrui.

Wicked Stepmother Nature (and you are,
or else you would have raised me better, with more
common sense), why did you give me such poor
judgment and self-control? Others are far

more shrewd than I. Two roads in a yellow wood,
and I take whichever is wrong and leads downhill,
attractive and easy, although I know well it will
not lead me to anything interesting or good.

And when I do exert myself and spend
my energies, it's not to some worthwhile end,
but only to help some stranger gain riches and fame.

I wear myself out and demonstrate what I can do,
but I don't even get any thanks for it when I'm through.
And when somebody else screws up, I get the blame.

Si par peine et sueur et par fidélité,
Par humble servitude et longue patience,
Employer corps et biens, esprit et conscience,
Et du tout mépriser sa propre utilité,

Si pour n'avoir jamais par importunité
Demandé bénéfice ou autre récompense,
On se doit enrichir, j'aurai (comme je pense)
Quelque bien à la fin, car je l'ai mérité.

Mais si par larcin avancé l'on doit être,
Par mentir, par flatter, par abuser son maître,
Et pis que tout cela faire encor bien souvent:

Je connais que je sème au rivage infertile,
Que je veux cribler l'eau, et que je bats le vent,
Et que je suis, Vineus, serviteur inutile.

If taking many pains and spending sweat
during long years of humble service counts,
and pouring out your lifeblood in amounts
that leave you drained, what profit do you get,

except by whining and wheedling, bowing and fawning,
laughing at stupid jokes, going down on your knees
to fools, and smiling, and saying "Pretty please!"?
You'd think I'd prosper, Vineus. But it's dawning

upon me that lying is how it's done, and stealing,
and rather worse than that—and I'm not revealing
secrets or pointing the finger. I admit, yes,

that I've sown my seed in a desert, wasted my time,
carried water in sieves, spat into the wind, and I'm
not only a clerk but a master of uselessness.

Si onques de pitié ton âme fut atteinte,
Voyant indignement ton ami tourmenté,
Et si onques tes yeux ont expérimenté
Les poignants aiguillons d'une douleur non feinte,

Vois la mienne en ces vers sans artifice peinte,
Comme sans artifice est ma simplicité:
Et si pour moi tu n'es à pleurer incité,
Ne te ris pour le moins des soupirs de ma plainte.

Ainsi, mon cher Vineus, jamais ne puisses-tu
Éprouver les regrets qu'éprouve une vertu
Qui se voit défrauder du loyer de sa peine:

Ainsi l'œil de ton roi favorable te soit,
Et ce qui des plus fins l'espérance déçoit,
N'abuse ta bonté d'une promesse vaine.

If ever pity has managed to touch your heart
at seeing your friend so badly used, if your
eyes could see my weeping, you'd know in these poor
performances I am not merely playing a part.

The pain is real, although the verse conceals
the rawness of it. Believe me, and do not burst
out laughing. The verse is second. The pain comes first,
if, mostly, artifice hides how bad it feels.

I hope, Vineus, that you may never know
the disappointments I've felt being treated so
badly by those for whom I've labored forever.

May the king himself reward you and may he see
your worth and proclaim it! And may you never be
cheated as people can be, no matter how clever.

O combien est heureux qui n'est contraint de feindre,
Ce que la vérité le contraint de penser,
Et à qui le respect d'un qu'on n'ose offenser
Ne peut la liberté de sa plume contraindre!

Las, pourquoi de ce nœud sens-je la mienne éteindre,
Quand mes justes regrets je cuide commencer?
Et pourquoi ne se peut mon âme dispenser
De ne sentir son mal ou de s'en pouvoir plaindre?

On me donne la gêne, et si n'ose crier,
On me voit tourmenter, et si n'ose prier
Qu'on ait pitié de moi. O peine trop sujette!

Il n'est feu si ardent qu'un feu qui est enclos,
Il n'est si fâcheux mal qu'un mal qui tient à l'os,
Et n'est si grand douleur qu'une douleur muette.

How happy is that man who is not required
to hide the thoughts that the truths of life propose
to his heart, and who need not lie or flatter those
of wealth or rank and title. I am heartily tired

of this knot about my heart, this yoke I wear
that all but strangles me. You'd think I'd become
accustomed to it, learning what all the dumb
beasts must learn at last, which is how to bear

the pain and not cry out in their agony. I
am put to the rack and think that I must die,
while people ignore my suffering, this mask

of tragedy I wear. The hottest fire
is one that's enclosed. The pain is deep and dire
when it's in the bone, needs pity, and cannot ask.

Si après quarante ans de fidèle service
Que celui que je sers a fait en divers lieux,
Employant, libéral, tout son plus et son mieux
Aux affaires qui sont de plus digne exercice,

D'un haineux étranger l'envieuse malice
Exerce contre lui son courage odieux,
Et sans avoir souci des hommes ni des dieux,
Oppose à la vertu l'ignorance et le vice,

Me dois-je tourmenter, moi, qui suis moins que rien,
Si par quelqu'un (peut-être) envieux de mon bien
Je ne trouve à mon gré la faveur opportune?

Je me console donc, et en pareille mer,
Voyant mon cher seigneur au danger d'abîmer,
Il me plaît de courir une même fortune.

If after forty years of faithful service,
the one I serve has striven in various places,
expending himself in all kinds of wild-goose chases
he thought would repay us both as we deserve, is

this how it is? He is abused, reviled
by envious foreigners who bear a grudge
and do not fear how God in heaven will judge
but plot against him as if he were a child

of the devil. But what's it to me? And why should I care
if my master is treated badly? I've been there,
done that, shot it, ate it. And watching him,

I see how the world works more often than not.
In that sea I've often thrashed in, he has got
to swallow salty water or learn to swim.

Sortons, Dilliers, sortons, faisons place à l'envie,
Et fuyons désormais ce tumulte civil,
Puisqu'on y voit priser le plus lâche et plus vil,
Et la meilleure part être la moins suivie.

Allons où la vertu et le sort nous convie,
Dussions-nous voir le Scythe ou la source du Nil,
Et nous donnons plutôt un éternel exil,
Que tacher d'un seul point l'honneur de notre vie.

Sus donques, et devant que le cruel vainqueur
De nous fasse une fable au vulgaire moqueur,
Bannissons la vertu d'un exil volontaire.

Et quoi? ne sais-tu pas que le banni romain,
Bien qu'il fût déchassé de son peuple inhumain,
Fut pourtant adoré du barbare corsaire?

Let us get out while we can, Dilliers, to make way
for envy that prompts the mob out there in the street.
Let's avoid these villains, admit defeat
and high-tail it somewhere else . . . Let us not stay

another moment but leave on the next tide
to Scythia or wherever—the source of the Nile—
some barbarous fastness for our eternal exile.
Thus may honor's demands be satisfied.

Let us be gone, then, before we are brought down
and become a butt of jokes throughout the town.
If the recognition of merit has fled, we two

should follow while we still can. Have we not learned
from Scipio how to behave when one is spurned
by the nasty mob? We're out of here. We're through.

Mauny, prenons en gré la mauvaise fortune,
Puisque nul ne se peut de la bonne assurer,
Et que de la mauvaise on peut bien espérer,
Étant son naturel de n'être jamais une.

Le sage nocher craint la faveur de Neptune,
Sachant que le beau temps longtemps ne peut durer:
Et ne vaut-il pas mieux quelque orage endurer,
Que d'avoir toujours peur de la mer importune?

Par la bonne fortune on se trouve abusé,
Par la fortune adverse on devient plus rusé:
L'une éteint la vertu, l'autre la fait paraître:

L'une trompe nos yeux d'un visage menteur,
L'autre nous fait l'ami connaître du flatteur,
Et si nous fait encore à nous-mêmes connaître.

Mauny, I say we ought to develop a taste
for our bad luck. Good fortune is never secure,
but with bad, you always know where you are, and you're
able to hope as well, so it's not a waste.

The experienced helmsman always looks with distrust
at fair weather, which he understands can't last.
When the storm is raging, the sail is furled, and the mast
creaks, it's better to smile at what you must

somehow endure. Good fortune's only a snare,
while ill luck teaches us how to prepare and take care.
One saps our strength; the other gives it. I ask

what's better? The one speaks fairly but tells us lies.
The other reveals our real friends to our eyes
and shows us what we are underneath the mask.

Si les larmes servaient de remède au malheur,
Et le pleurer pouvait la tristesse arrêter,
On devrait, Seigneur mien, les larmes acheter,
Et ne se trouverait rien si cher que le pleur.

Mais les pleurs en effet sont de nulle valeur:
Car soit qu'on ne se veuille en pleurant tourmenter,
Ou soit que nuit et jour on veuille lamenter,
On ne peut divertir le cours de la douleur.

Le cœur fait au cerveau cette humeur exhaler,
Et le cerveau la fait par les yeux dévaler,
Mais le mal par les yeux ne s'alambique pas.

De quoi donques nous sert ce fâcheux larmoyer?
De jeter, comme on dit, l'huile sur le foyer,
Et perdre sans profit le repos et repas.

If weeping were a remedy for grief
and tears could end one's sadness, then they'd be
worth more, Seigneur, than any king's treasury,
but the shedding of tears offers us no relief,

so it makes no difference at all whether you weep
day and night or are strong and stoic: the main
cure is time, for the heart sends up to the brain
a vapor that condenses again to seep

or pour down from the eyes, and this keeps going
until it stops and the tears are no longer flowing.
So what's the good of tears? They are useless, quite,

like trying to put out a fire by pouring oil.
It only burns the hotter, and meanwhile you spoil
your sleep at night and ruin your appetite.

Vivons, Gordes, vivons, vivons, et pour le bruit
Des vieillards ne laissons à faire bonne chère:
Vivons, puisque la vie est si courte et si chère,
Et que même les rois n'en ont que l'usufruit.

Le jour s'éteint au soir, et au matin reluit,
Et les saisons refont leur course coutumière:
Mais quand l'homme a perdu cette douce lumière,
La mort lui fait dormir une éternelle nuit.

Donc imiterons-nous le vivre d'une bête?
Non, mais devers le ciel levant toujours la tête,
Goûterons quelquefois la douceur du plaisir.

Celui vraiment est fol, qui changeant l'assurance
Du bien qui est présent en douteuse espérance,
Veut toujours contredire à son propre désir.

Let us live, Gordes, live, live, and dismay
old farts about whom we do not care, old sport,
for life is sweet and wonderful, and short,
and not even kings can keep it from slipping away.

Day gives way to night; a new day breaks;
and season gives way to the next as is customary.
Then death comes with its long sleep for the weary.
This happens also to beasts. But the wise man takes

whatever sweetness and pleasure may come to hand
along the way, because he can understand
that his time on earth is finite. Need I explain?

Only a fool would deny himself his share
of pleasure, for the vain hope that, elsewhere,
true happiness lies, and for its sake refrain.

Maraud, qui n'es maraud que de nom seulement,
Qui dit que tu es sage, il dit la vérité:
Mais qui dit que le soin d'éviter pauvreté
Te ronge le cerveau, ta face le dément.

Celui vraiment est riche et vit heureusement
Qui, s'éloignant de l'une et l'autre extrémité,
Prescrit à ses désirs un terme limité:
Car la vraye richesse est le contentement.

Sus donc, mon cher Maraud, pendant que notre maître,
Que pour le bien public la nature a fait naître,
Se tourmente l'esprit des affaires d'autrui,

Va devant à la vigne apprêter la salade:
Que sait-on qui demain sera mort ou malade?
Celui vit seulement, lequel vit aujourd'hui.

Maraud, you are not, despite your name's implication,
a marauder—you're a philosopher, serene,
not knocking your brains out every day in the keen
contest for money. And if your situation

were different, you'd look the same and behave the same
with money to burn. But you keep to the middle way,
allowing yourself restrained desires. They say
that always to be at ease is to win the game.

Come then, Maraud, and while our master scurries
on the public business, burdened with public worries,
and other people's affairs that crease his brow,

let us go out to the arbor and together
prepare a salad to eat in this pleasant weather,
for this is the place to live, and the time is now.

Montigné (car tu es aux procès usité)
Si quelqu'un de ces dieux, qui ont plus de puissance,
Nous promit de tous biens paisible jouissance,
Nous obligeant par Styx toute sa déité,

Il s'est mal envers nous de promesse acquitté,
Et devant Jupiter en devons faire instance:
Mais si l'on ne peut faire aux Parques résistance,
Qui jugent par arrêt de la fatalité,

Nous n'en appellerons, attendu que ne sommes
Plus privilégiés que sont les autres hommes
Condamnés, comme nous, en pareille action:

Mais si l'ennui voulait sur notre fantaisie,
Par vertu du malheur, faire quelque saisie,
Nous nous opposerons à l'exécution.

Montigné, you know about trials and the tricks
of the law: if some god, a powerful one, could give
his pledge that we'd both prosper in peace and live
comfortable lives, and swear by the mighty Styx,

we could take him to court. He hasn't performed at all
     well.
We might appeal to Jupiter, or if there's no
higher jurisdiction, no place to go,
in heaven, we'd just let it go. And what the hell!

We have no special immunities or rights,
and others have been found guilty and lost their fights
in similar cases. But if Ennui entered a plea,

as a friend of the court, to ask for a rehearing
and an order to end those troubles all mortals are bearing,
and we won—would we accept the judge's decree?

Baïf, qui, comme moi, prouves l'adversité,
Il n'est pas toujours bon de combattre l'orage,
Il faut caler la voile, et de peur du naufrage
Céder à la fureur de Neptune irrité.

Mais il ne faut aussi par crainte et vilité
S'abandonner en proie: il faut prendre courage,
Il faut feindre souvent l'espoir par le visage,
Et faut faire vertu de la nécessité.

Donques sans nous ronger le cœur d'un trop grand soin,
Mais de notre vertu nous aidant au besoin,
Combattons le malheur. Quant à moi, je proteste

Que je veux désormais fortune dépiter,
Et que si elle entreprend le me faire quitter,
Je le tiendrai, Baïf, et fût-ce de ma reste.

Baïf, you know adversity's power as well
as I do, and how one cannot fight the storm.
One must reef sail, heave to, or come to harm
as the winds whip the spray off the sea's swell.

But must one be a victim? A coward, taking
whatever comes without any struggle? No,
put on a brave face, when beleaguered so,
and summon your courage up, though you may be quaking

in your boots. We try to do the best we can,
in the struggle against Dame Fortune. Be a man.
What choice have we got? Hang in there until hope's gone.

She doesn't like it? Tough, let her lump it, then.
She may relent and change her tune, my friend.
Do what you can, Baïf. We'll carry on.

Cependant que tu suis le lièvre par la plaine,
Le sanglier par les bois et le milan par l'air,
Et que voyant le sacre ou l'épervier voler,
Tu t'exerces le corps d'une plaisante peine,

Nous autres malheureux suivons la cour romaine,
Où, comme de ton temps, nous n'oyons plus parler
De rire, de sauter, de danser et baller,
Mais de sang, et de feu, et de guerre inhumaine.

Pendant, tout le plaisir de ton Gorde et de moi,
C'est de te regretter et de parler de toi,
De lire quelque auteur ou quelque vers écrire.

Au reste, mon Dagaut, nous n'éprouvons ici
Que peine, que travail, que regret et souci,
Et rien, que Le Breton, ne nous peut faire rire.

What do you have to do but chase the hare
across the meadow or the wild boar in the wood,
or watch the kite in the air, or take the hood
from the falcon or sparrow hawk that will rise in the air

as you entertain yourself back there? In Rome
we do not laugh or talk of games or balls
but of blood and fire, savagery and brawls.
Your old friend Gordes and I miss you at home,

and take a wan pleasure in talking of you. I read
a book now and then, or write the odd poem. I need
some diversion from trouble and work, some cheer,

beyond our thoughts of you, Dagaut, whom we miss.
And Le Breton, at whom we still laugh, but this
is sad. It's a bad time. We're glad you're not here.

Le Breton est savant et sait fort bien écrire
En français et toscan, en grec et en romain,
Il est en son parler plaisant et fort humain,
Il est bon compagnon et dit le mot pour rire.

Il a bon jugement et sait fort bien élire
Le blanc d'avec le noir: il est bon écrivain,
Et pour bien compasser une lettre à la main,
Il y est excellent autant qu'on saurait dire.

Mais il est paresseux et craint tant son métier
Que s'il devait jeûner, ce crois-je, un mois entier,
Il ne travaillerait seulement un quart d'heure.

Bref il est si poltron, pour bien le deviser,
Que depuis quatre mois qu'en ma chambre il demeure,
Son ombre seulement me fait poltronniser.

Our friend Le Breton is a savant and knows how to write
in French and Tuscan, in Greek, and in Latin. A wit,
he can tell you a joke and make you laugh at it.
A funny guy, he can entertain you all night.

He's a sensible fellow too, who can tell the black
from the white, and it doesn't take him long. He can make
a shapely sentence without any spelling mistake.
In a word, he's as smart as a whip, sharp as a tack.

But he's lazy as sin and afraid of his own master.
He avoids his desk, and if, by some disaster,
he hadn't dined in a month, it would not be

enough to drive him to work for a quarter hour.
When I'm with him, his laziness has such power
that I yawn and feel my energies draining from me.

Tu ne me vois jamais, Pierre, que tu ne die
Que j'étudie trop, que je fasse l'amour,
Et que d'avoir toujours ces livres à l'entour
Rend les yeux éblouis et la tête alourdie.

Mais tu ne l'entends pas: car cette maladie
Ne me vient du trop lire ou du trop long séjour,
Ains de voir le bureau, qui se tient chacun jour:
C'est, Pierre mon ami, le livre où j'étudie.

Ne m'en parle donc plus, autant que tu as cher
De me donner plaisir et de ne me fâcher:
Mais bien en cependant que d'une main habile

Tu me laves la barbe et me tonds les cheveux,
Pour me désennuyer, conte-moi, si tu veux,
Des nouvelles du pape et du bruit de la ville.

You never see me, Pierre, without telling me I
should study a little less and make love more,
and it's books around my bed and on the floor
that trouble my eyes and give me a headache. Why

can you not understand? My indisposition
does not come from my reading too much or my stay
all this time in Rome; it's this slaving away
at my desk that's the real cause of my sorry condition.

As good a friend as you are, don't go on any longer,
if you really want to help me and make me stronger,
about how my life should be amended. Instead,

just give me another haircut, trim my beard,
and, to cure my boredom, tell me what scandals you've
     heard
and the news about whom the pope has taken to bed.

Seigneur, ne pensez pas d'ouïr chanter ici
Les louanges du roi, ni la gloire de Guise,
Ni celle que se sont les Châtillons acquise,
Ni ce temple sacré au grand Montmorency.

N'y pensez voir encor le sévère sourcil
De Madame Sagesse, ou la brave entreprise
Qui au ciel, aux démons, aux étoiles s'est prise,
La fortune, la mort, et la justice aussi,

De l'or encore moins, de lui je ne suis digne:
Mais bien d'un petit chat j'ai fait un petit hymne.
Lequel je vous envoie: autre présent je n'ai.

Prenez-le donc, Seigneur, et m'excusez, de grâce,
Si pour le bal ayant la musique trop basse,
Je sonne un passepied ou quelque branle gai.

Do not suppose, Seigneur, that in this I sing
of the king or the glory of Guise, or about the great
Chatillons, or the very large estate
that Montmorency has. This is no such thing,

nor is it a text where Philosophy knits her brow.
You won't learn much about heaven here, or the devil,
or the stars, or Fortune, or Death, or how Justice can level
rich and poor. And gold? No way, no how.

What you have here is praise of my pussycat—
which I send to you and hope you're pleased with that.
Accept it, my lord. If my gift is a modest one,

the fact is that I'm not much good at a ball
at court; I prefer a country dance and the small
pleasures a man can take there, if it's well done.

Qui est ami du cœur est ami de la bourse,
Ce dira quelque honnête et hardi demandeur,
Qui de l'argent d'autrui libéral dépendeur
Lui-même à l'hôpital s'en va toute la course.

Mais songe là-dessus qu'il n'est si vive source
Qu'on ne puisse épuiser, ni si riche prêteur
Qui ne puisse à la fin devenir emprunteur,
Ayant affaire à gens qui n'ont point de ressource.

Gordes, si tu veux vivre heureusement romain,
Sois large de faveur, mais garde que ta main
Ne soit à tous venants trop largement ouverte.

Par l'un on peut gagner même son ennemi,
Par l'autre bien souvent on perd un bon ami,
Et quand on perd l'argent, c'est une double perte.

A friend of the heart, they say, should be a friend
of the purse. But *they* are the ones who try to borrow
other people's money, and on the morrow
will be in the workhouse or come to an even worse end

in the river. But think: however abundant the spring,
it can exhaust itself, and a rich man can be
a borrower one day, having been so free
and open-handed. It's a most dangerous thing

you're doing, Gordes. In Rome, if you want to last,
you must teach yourself to be slow with your purse and fast
with fair words that can win you friends on the cheap.

Dipping into your pocket, all that you do
is put at risk the gold and the friendship, too,
both of which you might have been able to keep.

Ce rusé Calabrais tout vice, quel qu'il soit,
Chatouille à son ami, sans épargner personne,
Et faisant rire ceux que même il époinçonne,
Se joue autour du cœur de cil qui le reçoit.

Si donc quelque subtil en mes vers aperçoit
Que je morde en riant, pourtant nul ne me donne
Le nom de feint ami vers ceux que j'aiguillonne:
Car qui m'estime tel, lourdement se déçoit.

La satire, Dilliers, est un public exemple,
Où, comme en un miroir, l'homme sage contemple
Tout ce qui est en lui ou de laid ou de beau.

Nul ne me lise donc, ou qui me voudra lire
Ne se fâche s'il voit, par manière de rire,
Quelque chose du sien portrait en ce tableau.

The clever Latin poet talks of the vice
of his friends, and spares nobody in the cause
of getting that laugh he wants. And he always does—
from victims as well as everyone else. My advice

to readers, then, who see themselves here, is to smile,
as I do, myself. The attack shouldn't cancel out
a real friendship. That's not what this is about
(and we're smart enough to maintain a thought even while

we affirm its opposite). Satire, dear Dilliers,
is a mirror in which the wise can look, and they
can see how they are attractive or not: they need

an honest poet. Now and in time to come,
thin-skinned types may take offense at some
of the things I love to write that they hate to read.

» 63

Quel est celui qui veut faire croire de soi
Qu'il est fidèle ami, mais quand le temps se change,
Du côté des plus forts soudainement se range,
Et du côté de ceux qui ont le mieux de quoi?

Quel est celui qui dit qu'il gouverne le roi?
J'entends quand il se voit en un pays étrange,
Et bien loin de la cour: quel homme est-ce, Lestrange?
Lestrange, entre nous deux, je te pry, dis-le-moi.

Dis-moi, quel est celui qui si bien se déguise
Qu'il semble homme de guerre entre les gens d'église,
Et entre gens de guerre aux prêtres est pareil?

Je ne sais pas son nom: mais quiconque il puisse être
Il n'est fidèle ami, ni mignon de son maître,
Ni vaillant chevalier, ni homme de conseil.

Who is he who wants us to think him a good
friend, but then, when the wind shifts, shifts also,
makes tracks, contrives to turn his coat and go
to the winning side—as you always thought he would?

He hangs about with the rich. He claims he's got
the ear of the king, or anyway, will take
the chance when you and he are abroad to make
that easy boast. L'Estrange, perhaps? Is it not

he, do you think? Who else, between you and me,
could it be? Among the cassocked churchmen he
will pretend to be a soldier. And tit for tat,

among the soldiers, he'll say that he's a priest.
I've no idea who it is, haven't the least
notion. But do not trust him. Verbum sat.

Nature est aux bâtards volontiers favorable,
Et souvent les bâtards sont les plus généreux,
Pour être au jeu d'amour l'homme plus vigoureux,
D'autant que le plaisir lui est plus agréable.

Le dompteur de Méduse, Hercule l'indomptable,
Le vainqueur indien et les Jumeaux heureux,
Et tous ces dieux bâtards jadis si valeureux,
Ce problème, Bizet, font plus que véritable.

Et combien voyons-nous aujourd'hui de bâtards,
Soit en l'art d'Apollon, soit en celui de Mars,
Exceller ceux qui sont de race légitime?

Bref, toujours ces bâtards sont de gentil esprit:
Mais ce bâtard, Bizet, que l'on nous a décrit,
Est cause que je fais des autres moins d'estime.

Nature is often favorably inclined
to bastards, who can be more often than not
so full of life, perhaps having been begot
with more delight than fathers otherwise find

in the act of procreation. Theseus's case
comes to mind, and Hercules', and Bacchus's,
and Castor and Pollux's . . . Do all these myths mock us?
And what are the gods telling the human race?

Look at all the bastards we see, today,
who are doing so well as poets or soldiers, Bizet,
and compare them with legitimate offspring. Which

have talent, more noble minds? And yet I can name
one who, all on his own, refreshes the blame
that attaches to all bastards—that son of a bitch.

Tu ne crains la fureur de ma plume animée,
Pensant que je n'ai rien à dire contre toi,
Sinon ce que ta rage a vomi contre moi,
Grinçant comme un mâtin la dent envenimée.

Tu crois que je n'en sais que par la renommée,
Et que quand j'aurai dit que tu n'as point de foi,
Que tu es affronteur, que tu es traître au roi,
Que j'aurai contre toi ma force consommée,

Tu penses que je n'ai rien de quoi me venger,
Sinon que tu n'es fait que pour boire et manger:
Mais j'ai bien quelque chose encore plus mordante.

Et quoi? l'amour d'Orphée? et que tu ne sus onc
Que c'est de croire en Dieu? Non. Quel vice est-ce donc?
C'est, pour le faire court, que tu es un pédante.

You do not fear my animated pen,
believing there's nothing that I can say or do—
that I won't respond to the rage and vomit you spew,
grinding your teeth like a guard dog in his den.

You think it is only by repute I know you,
and that when I've said you're a lying, slanderous traitor
there's nothing left, no worse abuse or greater
insult to hurl at your head, but let me show you,

let me give you something to chew and swallow,
as you sit down to dine, for it wouldn't at all ring hollow
if I called you an atheist pederast. And I do,

but that doesn't begin to faze you. You hardly blink.
What vice, then, do you display that people think
is even worse? I'll say you're a pedant, too.

Ne t'émerveille point que chacun il méprise,
Qu'il dédaigne un chacun, qu'il n'estime que soi,
Qu'aux ouvrages d'autrui il veuille donner loi,
Et comme un Aristarq' lui-même s'autorise.

Paschal, c'est un pédant': et quoiqu'il se déguise,
Sera toujours pédant'. Un pédant' et un roi
Ne te semblent-ils pas avoir je ne sais quoi
De semblable, et que l'un à l'autre symbolise?

Les sujets du pédant', ce sont ses écoliers,
Ses classes ses états, ses régents officiers,
Son collège, Paschal, est comme sa province.

Et c'est pourquoi jadis le Syracusien,
Ayant perdu le nom de roi sicilien,
Voulut être pédant', ne pouvant être prince.

That he hates everyone he knows is no surprise,
nor treats men with contempt, and only admires
his own prose, to which the whole world aspires
(or so he supposes). He is, in his own eyes,

an absolute Aristarchus, his own ideal.
I tell you, Paschal, he is a pedant. And what
have pedants and kings in common? Rather a lot,
for neither believes that anyone else is real.

The pedant sees his scholars as subjects and his
classes as grand levees, while the college is
the government, the kingdom—which makes it clear

how the Syracusan Dionysus could,
when overthrown, decide that teaching was good
for a tyrant to take up as a second career.

Magny, je ne puis voir un prodigue d'honneur,
Qui trouve tout bien fait, qui de tout s'émerveille,
Qui mes fautes approuve et me flatte l'oreille,
Comme si j'étais prince ou quelque grand seigneur.

Mais je me fâche aussi d'un fâcheux repreneur,
Qui du bon et mauvais fait censure pareille,
Qui se lit volontiers, et semble qu'il sommeille
En lisant les chansons de quelque autre sonneur.

Celui-là me déçoit d'une fausse louange,
Et gardant qu'aux bons vers les mauvais je ne change,
Fait qu'en me plaisant trop à chacun je déplais:

Celui-ci me dégoûte, et ne pouvant rien faire
Qu'il lui plaise, il me fait également déplaire
Tout ce qu'il fait lui-même et tout ce que je fais.

Magny, I hate a fellow fulsome with praise
who oohs and aahs at everything in a delight
that gushes forth whether I'm wrong or right
in what I've done. But then, in opposite ways,

the nitpicker is odious, too, who finds
fault with anything, good or bad—his own
work excepted, of course, for that alone
delights him, and its defects he never minds.

To listen to the former is to lose
that chance to improve one might have put to use,
improving the work. He's bad, but even worse is

the latter, who's also useless, for nothing can
satisfy such a displeased, displeasing man,
and one learns to hate both him and one's own verses.

Je hais du Florentin l'usurière avarice,
Je hais du fol Siennois le sens mal arrêté,
Je hais du Genevois la rare vérité,
Et du Vénitien la trop caute malice:

Je hais le Ferrarais pour je ne sais quel vice,
Je hais tous les Lombards pour l'infidélité,
Le fier Napolitain pour sa grand' vanité,
Et le poltron romain pour son peu d'exercice:

Je hais l'Anglais mutin et le brave Écossais,
Le traître Bourguignon et l'indiscret Français,
Le superbe Espagnol et l'ivrogne Tudesque:

Bref, je hais quelque vice en chaque nation,
Je hais moi-même encor mon imperfection,
Mais je hais par sur tout un savoir pédantesque.

I hate the Florentines, usurious leeches;
I hate the Sienese, who are wild and crazy;
I hate the Genevans, whose notions of truth are hazy
at best, and Venetians, those cunning sons of bitches.

I hate Ferrarans, whose vices I can't even
imagine, and Lombards, who will always break
their promises, and Neapolitans, fake
arrogant peacocks . . . And Romans? That's a given!

The surly English and braggart Scots I despise.
Burgundians I hate for telling lies.
French yammer, Spaniards are vain, and the German
    drinks.

Each nation has its defect that wants correction.
And I hate myself for my own imperfection.
But what I hate worst is pedantry. That stinks.

Pourquoi me grondes-tu, vieux mâtin affamé,
Comme si du Bellay n'avait point de défense?
Pourquoi m'offenses-tu, qui ne t'ai fait offense,
Sinon de t'avoir trop quelquefois estimé?

Qui t'a, chien envieux, sur moi tant animé,
Sur moi, qui suis absent? crois-tu que ma vengeance
Ne puisse bien d'ici darder jusques en France
Un trait, plus que le tien, de rage enveminé?

Je pardonne à ton nom, pour ne souiller mon livre
D'un nom qui par mes vers n'a mérité de vivre:
Tu n'auras, malheureux, tant de faveur de moi.

Mais si plus longuement ta furcur persévère,
Je t'enverrai d'ici un fouet, une Mégère,
Un serpent, un cordeau, pour me venger de toi.

» 69

Why snap at me like a vicious junkyard cur?
You think du Bellay cannot reply or defend
himself against insults? Why and to what end?
I've never insulted you now, have I, sir—

except in my thoughts, which I've kept private. Do you
think, because I'm abroad and you're in France,
that you're safe from me and that there's not a chance
of any reply getting back to you? Yoo-hoo!

Here I am! But I won't write your name. I'll keep
that out, not to make you famous or my book cheap
and sordid by the mention of such a dope.

Just keep it up, though, and I'll contrive an answer
that I will somehow send back to you in France, sir,
to repay you—a poisonous snake, or a length of rope.

Si Pirithois ne fût aux enfers descendu,
L'amitié de Thésée serait ensevelie,
Et Nise par sa mort n'eût la sienne ennoblie,
S'il n'eût vu sur le champ Euryale étendu:

De Pylade le nom ne serait entendu
Sans la fureur d'Oreste, et la foi de Pythie
Ne fût par tant d'écrits en lumière sortie,
Si Damon ne se fût en sa place rendu:

Et je n'eusse éprouvé la tienne si muable,
Si fortune vers moi n'eût été variable.
Que puis-je faire donc, pour me venger de toi?

Le mal que je te veux, c'est qu'un jour je te puisse
Faire en pareil endroit, mais par meilleur office,
Reconnaître ta faute et voir quelle est ma foi.

If Pirithous had never descended to hell,
his friendship with Theseus would not now be famous.
And Nisus by his dying would not shame us,
unless he'd seen Euryalus as he fell.

Who would have heard of Pylades without
Orestes' fury, or Pythias's loyalty
without Damon's friendship? And we would be
legends, too, that poets could write about—

if you weren't such a fickle, fair-weather friend.
I've wished I could see you come to a wretched end,
or, better, I can imagine you in distress,

when you need me, when I'm helpful to you, and when
you see how a friend behaves to a friend—and then
I'll make you understand your worthlessness.

Ce brave qui se croit, pour un jaque de maille,
Être un second Roland, ce dissimulateur,
Qui superbe aux amis, aux ennemis flatteur,
Contrefait l'habile homme et ne dit rien qui vaille,

Belleau, ne le crois pas: et quoiqu'il se travaille
De se feindre hardi d'un visage menteur,
N'ajoute point de foi à son parler vanteur,
Car oncq homme vaillant je n'ai vu de sa taille.

Il ne parle jamais que des faveurs qu'il a:
Il dédaigne son maître, et courtise ceux-là
Qui ne font cas de lui: il brûle d'avarice:

Il fait du bon chrétien, et n'a ni foi ni loi:
Il fait de l'amoureux, mais c'est, comme je croi,
Pour couvrir le soupçon de quelque plus grand vice.

He thinks he can put on a coat of mail
and be a hero, a second Roland, as brave . . .
He's puffed up among his friends but a servile slave
to enemies; he's a flatterer, a pale

imitation, he thinks himself a treasure
of wit but what he says no one can recall.
His claims are laughable, Belleau. Do not fall
for that bluster of his but take his actual measure.

No man of any courage has such a mouth.
His name-dropping is foolish and uncouth.
He sneers at his betters and bullies whomever he can.

He's a hanger-on, greedy, smarmy, a snake,
who claims to be a Christian, for heaven's sake.
And he isn't a ladies'—but only a lady-*ish* man.

Encore que l'on eût heureusement compris
Et la doctrine grecque et la romaine ensemble,
Si est-ce, Gohory, qu'ici, comme il me semble,
On peut apprendre encor, tant soit-on bien appris.

Non pour trouver ici de plus doctes écrits
Que ceux que le français soigneusement assemble,
Mais pour l'air plus subtil, qui doucement nous emble
Ce qui est plus terrestre et lourd en nos esprits.

Je ne sais quel démon de sa flamme divine
Le moins parfait de nous purge, éprouve et affine,
Lime le jugement et le rend plus subtil:

Mais qui trop y demeure, il envoie en fumée
De l'esprit trop purgé la force consumée,
Et pour l'émoudre trop lui fait perdre le fil.

However much one excelled in Latin and Greek,
coming to Rome, Gohory, teaches what one
never learned in all those lessons he's done
so carefully. It isn't that one would seek

better libraries here than those of France.
It's the atmosphere here, the air, the weather. The spirit
that's still alive here speaks to those who come near it
and purifies our tempers and enchants.

Or is it perhaps a demon of some kind?
For if one stays too long, one's strength of mind
diminishes. Like Rome, we decline and fall.

The discipline we had as schoolboys is gone,
and we lose that youthful ambition that drove us on,
which seems amusing if not quite beyond recall.

Gordes, j'ai en horreur un vieillard vicieux
Qui l'aveugle appétit de la jeunesse imite,
Et jà froid par les ans de soi-même s'incite
A vivre délicat en repos otieux.

Mais je ne crains rien tant qu'un jeune ambitieux
Qui pour se faire grand contrefait de l'hermite,
Et voilant sa traïson d'un masque d'hypocrite,
Couve sous beau semblant un cœur malicieux.

Il n'est rien (ce dit-on en proverbe vulgaire)
Si sale qu'un vieux bouc, ni si prompt à mal faire
Comme est un jeune loup: et, pour le dire mieux,

Quand bien au naturel de tous deux je regarde,
Comme un fangeux pourceau l'un déplaît à mes yeux,
Comme d'un fin renard de l'autre je me garde.

Gordes, I have a horror of dirty old men
who pretend to the blind desires of hot youth,
although their blood has cooled, to tell the truth,
and their lust is mostly an act of will. But then

a young man with ambition is frightening, too,
who gets himself up like a hermit, or pretends
to be an ascetic, or charms you for his ends,
to get ahead and get what he wants out of you.

An old goat, or a young wolf? Which do we choose?
Neither one is attractive. That's no news.
But look again. Look harder. Really stare

at the beasts, and they're transformed—a filthy swine,
which all of us find disgusting and malign,
and a sly fox, the more dangerous of the pair.

Tu dis que Du Bellay tient réputation,
Et que de ses amis il ne tient plus de compte:
Si ne suis-je seigneur, prince, marquis ou comte,
Et n'ai changé d'état ni de condition.

Jusqu'ici je ne sais que c'est d'ambition,
Et pour ne me voir grand ne rougis point de honte:
Aussi ma qualité ne baisse ni ne monte,
Car je ne suis sujet qu'à ma complexion.

Je ne sais comme il faut entretenir son maître,
Comme il faut courtiser, et moins quel il faut être
Pour vivre entre les grands, comme on vit aujourd'hui.

J'honore tout le monde et ne fâche personne:
Qui me donne un salut, quatre je lui en donne:
Qui ne fait cas de moi, je ne fais cas de lui.

You say du Bellay cares about reputation
more than about his friends? It is not so.
I'm no seigneur, or prince, or count. I have no
such titles or honors. I know my place and station,

which hasn't changed. And I have no ambition.
I'm not at all ashamed that I'm not a noble.
I do not fall or rise on fortune's bubble.
It's on my temperament that my condition

depends, and I have never learned to fawn
on a master, as one must if he wants to get on.
With grandees, I never know what to say or do.

To the whole world, I'm polite and respond in kind
to courtesies, but slights I never mind:
if someone ignores me, I ignore him, too.

Gordes, que Du Bellay aime plus que ses yeux,
Vois comme la nature, ainsi que du visage,
Nous a faits différents de mœurs et de courage,
Et ce qui plaît à l'un, à l'autre est odieux.

Tu dis: Je ne puis voir un sot audacieux
Qui un moindre que lui brave à son avantage,
Qui s'écoute parler, qui farde son langage,
Et fait croire de lui qu'il est mignon des dieux.

Je suis tout au contraire, et ma raison est telle:
Celui dont la douleur courtoisement m'appelle,
Me fait outre mon gré courtisan devenir:

Mais de tel entretien le brave me dispense:
Car n'étant obligé vers lui de récompense,
Je le laisse tout seul lui-même entretenir.

Gordes, you are a splendid fellow, but you
and I differ by nature, it can't be denied.
What one of us likes, the other cannot abide.
For braggarts and fools, for instance, you will make few

allowances. You hate men who put on airs
or dress up and show off like strutting whores,
or those who talk just to hear themselves, or the bores
who confess—or boast—of their crimes and their affairs.

My tastes are different. With those who try to be charming
I become, despite myself, polite, disarming,
a courtier almost. But those braggarts, who fill

your heart with loathing—whose names I need not
    mention—
cause me no trouble at all. Who pays attention?
You just keep quiet and let them talk. And they will.

Cent fois plus qu'à louer on se plaît à médire:
Pour ce qu'en médisant on dit la vérité,
Et louant, la faveur, ou bien l'autorité,
Contre ce qu'on en croit, fait bien souvent écrire.

Qu'il soit vrai, pris-tu onc tel plaisir d'ouïr lire
Les louanges d'un prince ou de quelque cité,
Qu'ouïr un Marc Antoine à mordre exercité
Dire cent mille mots qui font mourir de rire?

S'il est donques permis, sans offense d'aucun,
Des mœurs de notre temps deviser en commun,
Quiconque me lira m'estime fol ou sage:

Mais je crois qu'aujourd'hui tel pour sage est tenu,
Qui ne serait rien moins que pour tel reconnu,
Qui lui aurait ôté le masque du visage.

Bad-mouthing people is more delightful by far
than praising them, if only because that lets you
tell the truth for a change, while praising gets you
into that tight corner where either you are

a flattering liar or else are stricken dumb.
And even when praise is true, your reader is
bored. Who wants to read of some great man and his
decency and kindness? But broadcast some

scandal, some scurrilous joke at someone's expense,
and you are an instant success. It makes good sense
to talk about general vice, then, in general rages

that mention no names. The readers may think me a nut
or sane as they like, or even wise. But what
would they say if they recognized themselves on these
    pages?

Je ne découvre ici les mystères sacrés
Des saints prêtres romains, je ne veux rien écrire
Que la vierge honteuse ait vergogne de lire,
Je veux toucher sans plus aux vices moins secrets.

Mais tu diras que mal je nomme ces Regrets,
Vu que le plus souvent j'use de mots pour rire:
Et je dis que la mer ne bruit toujours son ire,
Et que toujours Phœbus ne sagette les Grecs.

Si tu rencontres donc ici quelque risée,
Ne baptise pourtant de plainte déguisée
Les vers que je soupire au bord ausonien.

La plainte que je fais, Dilliers, est véritable:
Si je ris, c'est ainsi qu'on se rit à la table,
Car je ris, comme on dit, d'un ris sardonien.

Sacred Vatican secrets? Some scandalous tale
of the priests in Rome? No, sir, that's not my style
at all. What I write would not make a virgin, while
she read these pages, blush, let alone turn pale.

The follies I am describing are all well known
and public. But why do I call the book *Regrets*
if, more than half the time, what a poem gets
is the readers' laughter? It's all a matter of tone.

The seas are not always choppy; the sun can shine.
And mixed up among these little poems of mine
are funny bits, Dilliers. When I make a moan,

it is real enough, but I am nonetheless able
to be amusing and even make the table
laugh—but its echo dies when I am alone.

Je ne te conterai de Bologne et Venise,
De Padoue et Ferrare et de Milan encor,
De Naples, de Florence, et lesquelles sont or
Meilleures pour la guerre ou pour la marchandise.

Je te raconterai du siège de l'Église,
Qui fait d'oisiveté son plus riche trésor,
Et qui dessous l'orgueil de trois couronnes d'or
Couve l'ambition, la haine et la feintise:

Je te dirai qu'ici le bonheur et malheur,
Le vice, la vertu, le plaisir, la douleur,
La science honorable et l'ignorance abonde.

Bref, je dirai qu'ici, comme en ce vieux chaos,
Se trouve, Peletier, confusément enclos
Tout ce qu'on voit de bien et de mal en ce monde.

Bologna, Venice, Padua, and Ferrara
I will not speak about, or Naples or
Milan, or which is best set up for war,
or which is best for a shopping spree or for a

holiday, but I'll write of this antic scene
in Rome, the church's headquarters, where under
the triple crown there is hatred, ambition (no wonder!),
pride, and pretense, and generous men and mean,

and learned and stupid rub shoulders, as virtue and vice
saunter through the piazzas together. It's nice,
the way they get on together here. Praying and sinning

can mix together, dear Pelletier, as we're told
the elements did in the tohu-and-bohu of old
in that Chaos they say obtained at the world's beginning.

Je n'écris point d'amour, n'étant point amoureux,
Je n'écris de beauté, n'ayant belle maîtresse,
Je n'écris de douceur, n'éprouvant que rudesse,
Je n'écris de plaisir, me trouvant douloureux:

Je n'écris de bonheur, me trouvant malheureux,
Je n'écris de faveur, ne voyant ma princesse,
Je n'écris de trésors, n'ayant point de richesse,
Je n'écris de santé, me sentant langoureux:

Je n'écris de la cour, étant loin de mon prince,
Je n'écris de la France, en étrange province,
Je n'écris de l'honneur, n'en voyant point ici:

Je n'écris d'amitié, ne trouvant que feintise,
Je n'écris de vertu, n'en trouvant point aussi,
Je n'écris de savoir, entre les gens d'Église.

I do not write of love: I am no lover.
I do not write of beauty: I have no woman.
I do not write of gentleness but the human
rudeness I see. And my pleasures are all over,

so I do not try to write of pleasure, but only
misery. Favors? No, I am on my own.
I do not write of riches: I have none.
Or of life at court, when I'm far from it and lonely.

I do not write of health, for I'm often ill.
I cannot write of France from a Roman hill.
Or honor? I see so little of that about.

I cannot write of friendship but only pretense.
I will not write of virtue, here in its absence.
Or knowledge or faith, in ignorance and doubt.

Si je monte au Palais, je n'y trouve qu'orgueil,
Que vice déguisé, qu'une cérémonie,
Qu'un bruit de tambourins, qu'une étrange harmonïe,
Et de rouges habits un superbe appareil:

Si je descends en banque, un amas et recueil
De nouvelles je trouve, une usure infinie,
De riches Florentins une troupe bannie,
Et de pauvres Siennois un lamentable deuil:

Si je vais plus avant, quelque part où j'arrive,
Je trouve de Vénus la grand bande lascive
Dressant de tous côtés mille appas amoureux:

Si je passe plus outre, et de la Rome neuve
Entre en la vieille Rome, adonques je ne treuve
Que de vieux monuments un grand monceau pierreux.

Whenever I go to the Vatican, I see
pride, vice in disguise, pomp on display
to the beating of massed drums, and every way
I look, rich scarlet habits in panoply.

If I go to the bourse, what I find there is also dismal:
expatriate Florentines or the somewhat less
rich Sienese near tears for their unsuccess
as they trade rumors and currencies. It's abysmal

everywhere I go in Rome. There are whores
who beckon bold as brass from open doors,
winking, leering, and ready to jump my bones.

And if I go farther and leave the new Rome behind,
the old Rome's no less depressing: there, I find
its once proud monuments fallen to heaps of stones.

Il fait bon voir, Paschal, un conclave serré,
Et l'une chambre à l'autre également voisine
D'antichambre servir, de salle et de cuisine,
En un petit recoin de dix pieds en carré:

Il fait bon voir autour le palais emmuré,
Et briguer là-dedans cette troupe divine,
L'un par ambition, l'autre par bonne mine,
Et par dépit de l'un être l'autre adoré:

Il fait bon voir dehors toute la ville en armes
Crier: le Pape est fait, donner de faux alarmes,
Saccager un palais: mais plus que tout cela

Fait bon voir, qui de l'un, qui de l'autre se vante,
Qui met pour celui-ci, qui met pour celui-là,
Et pour moins d'un écu dix cardinaux en vente.

It is wonderful fun, Paschal, to see them meet,
the cardinals in conclave, sardines packed
into their tiny cubicles, walled in, in fact,
whitewashed cells ten feet by perhaps ten feet,

and all these holy men are plotting and scheming,
deep in intrigue, ambitious, and full of guile.
If they're all jealous of one, another will smile
and imagine that he is the man of whom they're dreaming.

It's good to see how the Romans all watch for smoke.
Is a pope elected? Or is it perhaps a joke?
Or is someone just cooking pasta? In alleys they run,

chasing down rumors or maybe to place a bet.
Who benefits? Who loses? These days you can get
ten cardinals for the usual price of one.

Veux-tu savoir, Duthier, quelle chose c'est Rome?
Rome est de tout le monde un publique échafaud,
Une scène, un théâtre, auquel rien ne défaut
De ce qui peut tomber ès actions de l'homme.

Ici se voit le jeu de la fortune, et comme
Sa main nous fait tourner ores bas, ores haut:
Ici chacun se montre, et ne peut, tant soit caut,
Faire que tel qu'il est, le peuple ne le nomme.

Ici du faux et vrai la messagère court,
Ici les courtisans font l'amour et la cour,
Ici l'ambition et la finesse abonde:

Ici la liberté fait l'humble audacieux,
Ici l'oisiveté rend le bon vicieux,
Ici le vil faquin discourt des faits du monde.

You want to know, Duthier, what kind of place
Rome is? It's the world's great stage, on which is seen
and heard whatever can be or is or has been.
Here is the wheel of Fortune, and this is the place

where one may rise as another falls, and the sins
of each are plain for all to see, however
much he may try to conceal them and however clever
he thinks he is. But everyone knows, and grins.

Rumor travels fast, as the truth does too.
Diplomats have their affairs and courtiers screw,
and everyone is procuring with more or less

boldness and license, and idleness wins out,
unopposed in virtue's all but total rout
that cynical fools discuss in their shamelessness.

Ne pense, Robertet, que cette Rome-ci
Soit cette Rome-là qui te soulait tant plaire.
On n'y fait plus crédit, comme l'on soulait faire,
On n'y fait plus l'amour, comme on soulait aussi.

La paix et le bon temps ne règnent plus ici,
La musique et le bal sont contraints de s'y taire,
L'air y est corrompu, Mars y est ordinaire,
Ordinaire la faim, la peine, et le souci.

L'artisan débauché y ferme sa boutique,
L'otieux avocat y laisse sa pratique,
Et le pauvre marchand y porte le bissac:

On ne voit que soldats, et morions en tête,
On n'oit que tambourins et semblable tempête,
Et Rome tous les jours n'attend qu'un autre sac.

Do not suppose, dear Robertet, that the Rome
of today is at all like the city that you found
so pleasing once. It's changed, decayed, unsound.
Not even making love is the same. We've come

to a sorry state where the music is stilled and the dance
has stopped. The air is vile, and violence
is everywhere. Nothing makes any sense.
There's hunger, suffering, fear. The artisan wants

customers; the lawyer has let his practice
go; the merchant has shut his shop; and the fact is
his children beg on the streets, where nervous men

in uniforms and helmets are out on patrol.
We hear the trumpets' blare and the snare drums' roll
and fear—or hope—for Rome to be sacked again.

Nous ne faisons la cour aux filles de Mémoire,
Comme vous qui vivez libres de passion:
Si vous ne savez donc notre occupation,
Ces dix vers en suivant vous la feront notoire:

Suivre son cardinal au Pape, au Consistoire,
En Capelle, en Visite, en Congrégation,
Et pour l'honneur d'un prince ou d'une nation
De quelque ambassadeur accompagner la gloire:

Être en son rang de garde auprès de son seigneur,
Et faire aux survenants l'accoutumé honneur,
Parler du bruit qui court, faire de l'habile homme

Se promener en housse, aller voir d'huis en huis
La Marthe ou la Victoire, et s'engager aux Juifs:
Voilà, mes compagnons, les passe-temps de Rome.

We do not pay court to the Muses here and write
poetry as you do, living in ways
I envy. You want to know how I spend my days?
In the ten lines that are left, I will recite:

Follow one's cardinal to the pope or to
the consistory, the chapel, the congregation,
or to honor a prince or meet with some delegation,
or attend an ambassador's ceremonial do.

The master has his train, and one's place is in it.
You whisper to one, or you give another a minute
and talk of the latest rumors and try to appear

smart. You go from house to house to amuse
great courtesans or to borrow money from Jews.
That's life in Rome. That's how I pass time here.

Flatter un créditeur, pour son terme allonger,
Courtiser un banquier, donner bonne espérance,
Ne suivre en son parler la liberté de France,
Et pour répondre un mot, un quart d'heure y songer:

Ne gâter sa santé par trop boire et manger,
Ne faire sans propos une folle dépense,
Ne dire à tous venants tout cela que l'on pense,
Et d'un maigre discours gouverner l'étranger:

Connaître les humeurs, connaître qui demande,
Et d'autant que l'on a la liberté plus grande,
D'autant plus se garder que l'on ne soit repris:

Vivre avecques chacun, de chacun faire compte:
Voilà, mon cher Morel (dont je rougis de honte),
Tout le bien qu'en trois ans à Rome j'ai appris.

To flatter creditors and somehow stall for more
time; to appear more prosperous to create
a good impression on bankers; never to state
freely what one believes as one did before

in France; to avoid getting drunk or overeating;
not to be free with one's purse; not to express
without much calculation one's views; to address,
lacking the words, those foreigners one is meeting;

to know who'll do what and who desires what;
to be more guarded, the more one knows, and shut
one's mouth; to listen, nod, smile, and keep mum;

to hobnob with one's enemies and to stay
on guard with friends: Morel, I'm ashamed to say
these are the things I've learned in three years in Rome.

Marcher d'un grave pas et d'un grave sourcil,
Et d'un grave sourire à chacun faire fête,
Balancer tous ses mots, répondre de la tête,
Avec un *Messer non,* ou bien un *Messer si:*

Entremêler souvent un petit *Et cosi,*
Et d'un *son Servitor'* contrefaire l'honnête,
Et, comme si l'on eût sa part en la conquête,
Discourir sur Florence, et sur Naples aussi:

Seigneuriser chacun d'un baisement de main,
Et, suivant la façon du courtisan romain,
Cacher sa pauvreté d'une brave apparence:

Voilà de cette cour la plus grande vertu,
Dont souvent mal monté, malsain, et mal vêtu,
Sans barbe et sans argent on s'en retourne en France.

To walk with a solemn look at a stately pace
and with a subtle smile greet every man;
to weigh one's words as carefully as one can,
with "Yes, sir," and "No, sir," thrown in as grace

notes, or else an "*E così*," or "Your
servant, sir," and to fake sincerity;
to speak of Florence and Naples and to be
optimistic about the chances for

a victory; to treat each man as a lord
and kiss his hand, and never to seem bored,
but attentive to any Roman courtier's glance;

to hide one's poverty with showy clothing
(that's all they value here) . . . And then, with loathing,
impoverished, broken, slink back home to France.

D'où vient cela, Mauny, que tant plus on s'efforce
D'échapper hors d'ici, plus le démon du lieu
(Et que serait-ce donc, si ce n'est quelque dieu?)
Nous y tient attachés par une douce force?

Serait-ce point d'amour cette alléchante amorce,
Ou quelque autre venin, dont après avoir beu
Nous sentons nos esprits nous laisser peu à peu,
Comme un corps qui se perd sous une neuve écorce?

J'ai voulu mille fois de ce lieu m'étranger,
Mais je sens mes cheveux en feuilles se changer,
Mes bras en longs rameaux, et mes pieds en racine.

Bref, je ne suis plus rien qu'un vieux tronc animé,
Qui se plaint de se voir à ce bord transformé,
Comme le myrte anglais au rivage d'Alcine.

How could it come to pass, Mauny, that for all
our efforts to escape this place, it pulls
us back? Is it some mischievous god who fools
with our destinies and holds us here in thrall?

Can it be love that keeps us here, or some other
poison we have drunk, that affects the mind,
and the skin and the brain shrivel, and one goes blind?
A thousand times I've said that I would rather

leave, but I feel my hair sprouting into leaf
and my arms turning into branches, and in the turf
my toes are becoming roots. I'm a damned tree

like that Englishman in *Orlando Furioso*.
Am I, too, bewitched by Alcina? I suppose so.
It happened to poor Ruggiero, and now to me.

Qui choisira pour moi la racine d'Ulysse?
Et qui me gardera de tomber au danger
Qu'une Circe en pourceau ne me puisse changer,
Pour être à tout jamais fait esclave du vice?

Qui m'étreindra le doigt de l'anneau de Mélisse,
Pour me désenchanter comme un autre Roger?
Et quel Mercure encor me fera déloger,
Pour ne perdre mon temps en l'amoureux service?

Qui me fera passer sans écouter la voix
Et la feinte douceur des monstres d'Achelois?
Qui chassera de moi ces Harpies friandes?

Qui volera pour moi encore un coup aux cieux,
Pour rapporter mon sens et me rendre mes yeux?
Et qui fera qu'en paix je mange mes viandes?

Who will find me that moly that kept Ulysses
safe and that might protect me from Circe's spell?
Without it, I fear I'm going straight to hell,
having succumbed to the lure of temptresses' kisses.

Who will put Melissa's magic ring
that she gave to Ruggiero on my finger?
Will the god Mercury come to my aid to bring a
release from love? I hear the Sirens sing,

and greedy Harpies gather before my eyes.
Who will drive them away, or from out of the skies
steal thunderbolts to make me like other men?

I want what I can barely remember—peace
and quiet. I was once content with these.
How can I know such happiness again?

Gordes, il m'est avis que je suis éveillé,
Comme un qui tout ému d'un effroyable songe
Se réveille en sursaut et par le lit s'allonge,
S'émerveillant d'avoir si longtemps sommeillé.

Roger devint ainsi (ce crois-je) émerveillé:
Et crois que tout ainsi la vergogne me ronge,
Comme lui, quand il eut découvert le mensonge
Du fard magicien qui l'avait aveuglé.

Et comme lui aussi je veux changer de style,
Pour vivre désormais au sein de Logistille,
Qui des cœurs langoureux est le commun support.

Sus donc, Gordes, sus donc, à la voile, à la rame,
Fuyons, gagnons le haut, je vois le belle Dame
Qui d'un heureux signal nous appelle à son port.

Gordes, I have been woken from a deep
slumber, frightened, roused by a terrible dream
the way you can be, and the echo of my scream
still hangs in the air and the cold sweat from my sleep

is not yet dry. Ruggiero in just this way
was struck with wonder: I, too, to my shame,
discover my life has been a dishonest game
that only a villain or fool would want to play.

Like him, I want to change my life and station
and be with Logistilla, that incarnation
of noble ideals all good men should prefer.

Hoist the sail then, Gordes, seize the oar,
and let us make haste to quit this wretched shore.
The belle Dame summons; we must go to her.

Ne pense pas, Bouju, que les nymphes latines
Pour couvrir leur traïson d'une humble privauté,
Ni pour masquer leur teint d'une fausse beauté,
Me fassent oublier nos nymphes angevines.

L'angevine douceur, les paroles divines,
L'habit qui ne tient rien de l'impudicité,
La grâce, la jeunesse et la simplicité
Me dégoûtent, Bouju, de ces vieilles Alcines.

Qui les voit par-dehors ne peut rien voir plus beau,
Mais le dedans ressemble au dedans d'un tombeau,
Et si rien entre nous moins honnête se nomme.

O quelle gourmandise! ô queile pauvreté!
O quelle horreur de voir leur immondicité!
C'est vraiment de les voir le salut d'un jeune homme.

Don't think, Bouju, that the Latin nymphs who disguise
their treasons in a deceitful, humble mien
and cover their complexions with a sheen
of artifice can make me forget the eyes

of the even lovelier nymphs of Anjou and
their sweetness, gentle speech, appealing dress,
their Angevin grace and charming girlishness.
Compare them, Bouju, to this harridan band!

Their beauty is external—like that of a tomb,
inside which there's a rotten stench and gloom.
To desire them a man must be quite depraved.

How squalid, filthy, and vile they are. In truth,
though they may tempt an ignorant, innocent youth,
if he takes a good long look at them, he'll be saved.

O beaux cheveux d'argent mignonnement retors!
O front crêpe et serein! et vous, face dorée!
O beaux yeux de cristal! ô grand bouche honorée,
Qui d'un large repli retrousses tes deux bords!

O belles dents d'ébène! ô précieux trésors,
Qui faites d'un seul ris toute âme enamourée!
O gorge damasquine en cent plis figurée!
Et vous, beaux grands tétins, dignes d'un si beau corps!

O beaux ongles dorés! ô main courte et grassette!
O cuisse délicate! et vous, jambe grossette,
Et ce que je ne puis honnêtement nommer!

O beau corps transparent! ô beaux membres de glace!
O divines beautés! pardonnez-moi, de grâce,
Si, pour être mortel, je ne vous ose aimer.

O lovely hair, silver and in a stern
chignon! O brow with corrugated creases!
O face of sunburned bronze with masterpieces
of glass eyes! O large mouth with a downward turn!

What would Petrarch say of those teeth, black
as ebony—a precious wood, I think—
and that smile provoking laughter or just a wink?
And the damascene throat where one can trace the track

of interesting textures! And huge hooters!
And the long fingernails on the short fingers that suitors
must learn to admire. And those great piano legs,

beneath a body beyond comparison . . .
(At any rate I haven't thought of one
to earn that embrace for which the whole world begs.)

En mille crespillons les cheveux se friser,
Se pincer les sourcils, et d'une odeur choisie
Parfumer haut et bas sa charnure moisie,
Et de blanc et vermeil sa face déguiser:

Aller de nuit en masque, en masque deviser,
Se feindre à tous propos être d'amour saisie,
Siffler toute la nuit par une jalousie,
Et par martel de l'un, l'autre favoriser:

Baller, chanter, sonner, folâtrer dans la couche,
Avoir le plus souvent deux langues en la bouche,
Des courtisanes sont les ordinaires jeux.

Mais quel besoin est-il que je te les enseigne?
Si tu les veux savoir, Gordes, et si tu veux
En savoir plus encor, demande à la Chassaigne.

Her hair is done up in frizzy ringlets. She plucks
her eyebrows and rubs expensive unguents all over
her body top to bottom to try to cover
its moldiness. On her face are expensive mucks

of various colors. At night, she wears a mask.
She's always falling in love, or at least pretends,
and whistles at night through the jalousies to friends—
or anyone at all for that matter—to ask

them in, to dance, sing, chatter, and romp in bed.
She speaks, as they say, with two tongues in her head.
These are the games that whores and courtesans play?

I don't have to tell you, Gordes. You're not slow.
If you need any further confirmation, go
ask la Chassaigne; hear what he has to say.

Douce mère d'amour, gaillarde Cyprienne,
Qui fais sous ton pouvoir tout pouvoir se ranger,
Et qui des bords de Xanthe à ce bord étranger
Guidas avec ton fils ta gent dardanienne,

Si je retourne en France, ô mère idalienne,
Comme je vins ici, sans tomber au danger
De voir ma vieille peau en autre peau changer,
Et ma barbe française en barbe italienne,

Dès ici je fais vœu d'apprendre à ton autel,
Non le lis, ou la fleur d'amarante immortel,
Non cette fleur encor de ton sang colorée:

Mais bien de mon menton la plus blonde toison,
Me vantant d'avoir fait plus que ne fit Jason
Emportant le butin de la toison dorée.

O Venus, goddess of Cyprus, whose power all
other powers acknowledge, you helped your dear
son when from Scamander he came here.
Help me to journey back to France. I call

in supplication, lady of Ida. Be nice.
If I can get home safely, I solemnly swear
to shave off this Italian beard I wear
and lay it upon your altar in sacrifice.

You don't need any lilies; you wouldn't want
the immortal Amaranthus; and you can't
like flowers the color of blood. Better than these

I'll bring you a gift of the kind that Jason carried,
when he returned home with the woman he had married:
I'll match it and offer up another fleece.

Heureux celui qui peut longtemps suivre la guerre
Sans mort, ou sans blessure, ou sons longue prison!
Heureux qui longuement vit hors de sa maison
Sans dépendre son bien ou sans vendre sa terre!

Heureux qui peut en cour quelque faveur acquerre
Sans crainte de l'envie ou de quelque traïson!
Heureux qui peut longtemps sans danger de poison
Jouir d'un chapeau rouge ou des clefs de saint Pierre!

Heureux qui sans péril peut la mer fréquenter!
Heureux qui sans procès le palais peut hanter!
Heureux qui peut sans mal vivre l'âge d'un homme!

Heureux qui sans souci peut garder son trésor,
Sa femme sans soupçon, et plus heureux encor
Qui a pu sans peler vivre trois ans à Rome!

Happy is he who can go to war and fight
and not get taken prisoner and not be
killed or wounded. Happy, likewise, is he
who can leave his home and not lose his birthright.

Happy is he who can at court be given
some favor without arousing others' ire
or envy. Happy is he who avoids the dire
risks of poison that drips from the keys of heaven

hanging out with the red hats. Happy too
is the man who at sea is not in danger or who
has no Vatican lawsuits endlessly stalled.

Happy's the man who dies in his bed at peace,
with his dear wife. And he's happy as any of these
who lives in Rome three years and doesn't go bald.

Maudit soit mille fois le Borgne de Libye,
Qui, le cœur des rochers perçant de part en part,
Des Alpes renversa le naturel rempart,
Pour ouvrir le chemin de France en Italie.

Mars n'eût empoisonné d'une éternelle envie
Le cœur de l'Espagnol et du Français soudard,
Et tant de gens de bien ne seraient en hasard
De venir perdre ici et l'honneur et la vie.

Le Français corrompu par le vice étranger
Sa langue et son habit n'eût appris à changer,
Il n'eût changé ses mœurs en une autre nature.

Il n'eût point éprouvé le mal qui fait peler,
Il n'eût fait de son nom la vérole appeler,
Et n'eût fait si souvent d'un buffle sa monture.

A thousand maledictions on the head
of Hannibal, who found a way to break
his way through the Alps to Italy—a mistake
(a catastrophe is what I should have said)

that others are tempted to make, and often do.
Those restless, envious men of France and Spain
who travel here might otherwise remain
at home and keep their lives and their honors, too.

The Frenchman corrupted by foreign vices wouldn't
turn his coat or live the way he shouldn't,
forgetting his morals, his character, his nation.

He would not be an easy butt of laughter,
the one the Roman whores named the pox after,
drunk in the gutter, an object of detestation.

O Déesse, qui peux aux princes égaler
Un pauvre mendiant qui n'a que la parole,
Et qui peux d'un grand roi faire un maître d'école,
S'il te plaît de son lieu le faire dévaler:

Je ne te prie pas de me faire enrôler
Au rang de ces messieurs que la faveur accole,
Que l'on parle de moi, et que mon renom vole
De l'aile dont tu fais ces grands princes voler:

Je ne demande pas mille et mille autres choses
Qui dessous ton pouvoir sont largement encloses,
Aussi je n'eus jamais de tant de biens souci.

Je demande sans plus que le mien on ne mange,
Et que j'aie bientôt une lettre de change,
Pour n'aller sur le buffle au départir d'ici.

O Goddess, who can turn a prince into
a beggar with nothing but words he can claim as his own,
who demoted a great king once from his throne
to a mere schoolmaster; Fortune, I don't ask you

to make me rich, and have my name enrolled
with the great, so that people talk of me with the awe
they have for the lords of the state, the church, and the law.
I don't ask for any of that, not even for gold,

(although you could, if you felt prompted now or
then to give me a little—it's in your power).
But I do ask that my name may still be spoken

after I'm gone, that it not be quite erased,
that the sheriffs do not hound me and I'm not chased
by creditors when I'm helpless, broke and broken.

Doulcin, quand quelquefois je vois ces pauvres filles
Qui ont le diable au corps, ou le semblent avoir,
D'une horrible façon corps et tête mouvoir,
Et faire ce qu'on dit de ces vieilles Sibylles:

Quand je vois les plus forts se retrouver débiles,
Voulant forcer en vain leur forcené pouvoir:
Et quand même j'y vois perdre tout leur savoir
Ceux qui sont en votre art tenus des plus habiles:

Quand effroyablement écrier je les oy,
Et quand le blanc des yeux renverser je leur voy,
Tout le poil me hérisse, et ne sais plus que dire.

Mais quand je vois un moine avecques son latin
Leur tâter haut et bas le ventre et le tétin,
Cette frayeur se passe, et suis contraint de rire.

Doulcin, sometimes when I see these poor possessed
girls, whom the devil torments, grimace perhaps
or twitch or shake as the Sibyls did, or collapse,
the strongest of them utterly weak, I'm distressed.

And I see their helpless physicians wondering why
their patients are troubled and trying to figure out
what to do, and they're fearful and full of doubt,
while the girls' eyes roll back in their heads and they cry.

My hair stands on end and I'm speechless, wondering
      what in
heaven's name it could mean. Then some monk spouting
      Latin
shows up to perform an exorcism, and while

I watch, he does his routine to cure their fits,
rubbing his hands on their faces, their asses, their tits,
and my terror abates. It's all I can do not to smile.

D'où vient que nous voyons à Rome si souvent
Ces garces forcener, et la plupart d'icelles
N'être vieilles, Ronsard, mais d'âge de pucelles,
Et se trouver toujours en un même couvent?

Qui parle par leur voix? quel démon leur défend
De répondre à ceux-là qui ne sont connus d'elles?
Et d'où vient que soudain on ne les voit plus telles,
Ayant une chandelle éteinte de leur vent?

D'où vient que les saints lieux telles fureurs augmentent?
D'où vient que tant d'esprits une seule tourmentent?
Et que sortant les uns, le reste ne sort pas?

Dis, je te prie, Ronsard, toi qui sais leurs natures,
Ceux qui fâchent ainsi ces pauvres créatures,
Sont-ils des plus hautains, des moyens, ou plus bas?

How can so many girls in Rome go mad,
most of them only children, or near enough?
What do you think, Ronsard? This is spooky stuff!
There's a single convent, said to be specially bad,

where it happens a lot. Who talks through these girls?
    What devil
commands them or forbids them, warning of evil
if they should speak to strangers? It's very sad.

Why in these holy places do they get worse?
And why do so many spirits collect there to curse
mere children? If one is cured, what about the rest?

Is it a joke, Ronsard? Are there really creatures
that come to bedevil these girls, perverting their natures?
And are they the vilest spirits? The middle? The best?

Quand je vais par la rue, où tant de peuple abonde,
De prêtres, de prélats, et de moines aussi,
De banquiers, d'artisans, et n'y voyant, ainsi
Qu'on voit dedans Paris, la femme vagabonde:

Pyrrhe, après le dégât de l'universelle onde,
Ses pierres (dis-je alors) ne sema point ici:
Et semble proprement, à voir ce peuple-ci,
Que Dieu n'y ait formé que la moitié du monde.

Car la dame romaine en gravité marchant,
Comme la conseillère ou femme du marchand
Ne s'y promène point, et n'y voit-on que celles

Qui se sont de la cour l'honnête nom donné:
Dont je crains quelquefois qu'en France retourné,
Autant que j'en verrai ne me ressemblent telles.

I wander through the streets here where people abound—
priests and prelates, a banker, a monk in black,
and after a while, I begin to notice the lack
of what one would see in Paris—no women around!

One would think, after Noah's flood, that Rome
had not quite been restored and God had merely
restocked half of the world. The custom, here, clearly,
is that wives and daughters of gentlemen stay at home.

The only women one sees on the streets are those
who walk the streets, the hookers in garish clothes.
And after a while one accepts this as normal. I fear

when I get home again, there's a good chance
it may take me time to readjust, and in France,
I'll treat the women as I have learned to do here.

Ursin, quand j'oy nommer de ces vieux noms romains,
De ces beaux noms connus de l'Inde jusqu'au More,
Non les grands seulement, mais les moindres encore,
Voire ceux-là qui ont les ampoules aux mains:

Il me fâche d'ouïr appeler ces vilains
De ces noms tant fameux, que tout le monde honore:
Et sans le nom chrétien, le seul nom que j'adore,
Voudrais que de tels noms on appelât nos saints.

Le mien surtout me fâche, et me fâche un Guillaume,
Et mille autres sots noms communs en ce royaume,
Voyant tant de faquins indignement jouir

De ces beaux noms de Rome et de ceux de la Grèce:
Mais par sur tout, Ursin, il me fâche d'ouïr
Nommer une Thaïs du nom d'une Lucrèce.

Ursin, when I hear the names of some old
Romans, these great cognomens famous from
the Tagus to the Indus, applied to some
utterly worthless rascal, my blood runs cold.

Those names that the whole world honored have declined
to parody. It's absurd. I'd rather have
our Christian saints whose names are noble and brave,
but "Christian" pardons a lot, and I don't mind.

My own name troubles me, and Guillaume, too,
("resolute helmet") and others one hears through
the course of a day. But great names of Rome and Greece

are silly, Ursin, making pretentious claims
to anyone who can read and who knows those names:
imagine a whore who calls herself Lucrece.

Que dirons-nous, Melin, de cette cour romaine,
Où nous voyons chacun divers chemins tenir,
Et aux plus hauts honneurs les moindres parvenir,
Par vice, par vertu, par travail, et sans peine?

L'un fait pour s'avancer une dépense vaine,
L'autre par ce moyen se voit grand devenir,
L'un par sévérité se sait entretenir,
L'autre gagne les cœurs par sa douceur humaine:

L'un pour ne s'avancer se voit être avancé,
L'autre pour s'avancer se voit désavancé,
Et ce qui nuit à l'un, à l'autre est profitable:

Qui dit que le savoir est le chemin d'honneur,
Qui dit que l'ignorance attire le bonheur:
Lequel des deux, Melin, est le plus véritable?

What are the rules, Melin? And how is it done
in the court at Rome to climb the greasy pole,
where the least-talented man can achieve his goal?
Vice can succeed. Or virtue. Hard work for one

will do it, or dumb luck for another. Money
will help, but I have seen men spend a lot
and get nowhere. Solemnity is what
suffices for some. Or simply kindness. It's funny.

Modesty often succeeds, or pushiness, but
what works well for this man, for that will not.
Competence, knowledge? They sound good, and yet

stupid charm has been known to do quite well.
It beats the hell out of me, and I can't tell
for the life of me, Melin, which is the better bet.

On ne fait de tout bois l'image de Mercure,
Dit le proverbe vieil: mais nous voyons ici
De tout bois faire pape, et cardinaux aussi,
Et vêtir en trois jours tout une autre figure.

Les princes et les rois viennent grands de nature:
Aussi de leurs grandeurs n'ont-ils tant de souci,
Comme ces dieux nouveaux, qui n'ont que le sourcil
Pour faire révérer leur grandeur, qui peu dure.

Paschal, j'ai vu celui qui naguère traînait
Toute Rome après lui, quand il se promenait,
Avecques trois valets cheminer par la rue:

Et traîner après lui un long orgueil romain
Celui de qui le père a l'ampoule en la main,
Et, l'aiguillon au poing, se courbe à la charrue.

They warn you not to take wooden nickels, but here
they can take a block of wood, or a blockhead
and make him a pope or cardinal robed in red,
and three days later, nobody thinks it's queer.

Princes and kings are used to grandeur and show,
which do not, therefore, drive them crazy, but these
so suddenly promoted nonentities
are dazzled by it. I have seen great men go

alone through the streets of Rome whose names strike awe
in every person's heart and whose word is law.
That happens. What is harder to explain

is how it befalls that one of these upstarts passes,
whose father, a plowman, stared into his oxen's asses,
preceded by pages and followed now by a train.

» 103

Si la perte des tiens, si les pleurs de ta mère,
Et si de tes parents les regrets quelquefois,
Combien, cruel Amour, que sans amour tu sois,
T'ont fait sentir le deuil de leur complainte amère:

C'est or qu'il faut montrer ton flambeau sans lumière,
C'est or qu'il faut porter sans flèches ton carquois,
C'est or qu'il faut briser ton petit arc turquois,
Renouvelant le deuil de ta perte première.

Car ce n'est pas ici qu'il te faut regretter
Le père au bel Ascagne: il te faut lamenter
Le bel Ascagne même, Ascagne, ô quel dommage!

Ascagne, que Caraffe aimait plus que ses yeux:
Ascagne, qui passait en beauté de visage
Le beau coupier troyen qui verse à boire aux dieux.

You know what grief is, Cupid. Think of your mother,
Venus, mourning Aeneas. This is a day,
however cruel you are, to put away
your torch and arrows, as once you did for your brother,

and break your bow, for poor Ascanius's sake,
not your nephew, Aeneas's son, but this
sweet lad Caraffa loved and will sorely miss—
our Ascanius. The cardinal's heart may break

for the loss of this gorgeous boy, his toy, his pet,
as pretty as any Ganymede can get,
that Trojan cupbearer who poured the wine

for Olympus's gods. No one is safe from you.
You've had your triumph; now have pity, too.
That boy was really something. I'd call it divine.

Si fruits, raisins et blés, et autres telles choses,
Ont leur tronc, et leur cep, et leur semence aussi,
Et s'on voit au retour du printemps adouci
Naître de toutes parts violettes et roses:

Ni fruits, raisins, ni blés, ni fleurettes décloses
Sortiront, viateur, du corps qui gît ici:
Aulx, oignons, et porreaux, et ce qui fleure ainsi,
Auront ici dessous leurs semences encloses.

Toi donc, qui de l'encens et du baume n'as point,
Si du grand Jules tiers quelque regret te point,
Parfume son tombeau de telle odeur choisie:

Puisque son corps, qui fut jadis égal aux dieux,
Se soulait paître ici de tels mets précieux,
Comme au ciel Jupiter se paît de l'ambroisie.

If fruit and grapes and wheat and such manner of things
have shoots and stems, they surely have seeds, too,
and, when the gentle spring comes around, the new
violets come into bloom, but the season brings

no fruit or grape or wheat from this bit of dust.
Garlic, onions, and such modest crops will sprout,
if anything does, from the body that's here laid out.
The respect we owe this pope, passerby, we must

offer—but not with spice, which would be absurd.
On earth he was a glutton; now Julius the Third
has gone to that high table in the sky,

to be with his forebears or else to be
a part of that onion family that he
was always closer to, only heaven knows why.

De voir mignon du roi un courtisan honnête,
Voir un pauvre cadet l'ordre au col soutenir,
Un petit compagnon aux états parvenir,
Ce n'est chose, Morel, digne d'en faire fête.

Mais voir un estafier, un enfant, une bête,
Un forfant, un poltron cardinal devenir,
Et pour avoir bien su un singe entretenir
Un Ganymède avoir le rouge sur la tête:

S'être vu par les mains d'un soldat espagnol
Bien haut sur une échelle avoir la corde au col
Celui que par le nom de Saint-Père l'on nomme:

Un bélître en trois jours aux princes s'égaler,
Et puis le voir de là en trois jours dévaler:
Ces miracles, Morel, ne se font point, qu'à Rome.

To see the catamite of the king preferred,
a boy with orders and decorations, is not
so shocking, Morel. And a pension? We have got
to accept it; it can happen. But what's absurd

is when some page, some idiot, some child
is given a red hat. What are we to make
of that? He's got a monkey, for heaven's sake,
that they could have made a cardinal too. It's wild.

There was a fellow about to be beheaded,
was up there on the scaffold . . . I swear, I read it!
And they brought him down and elected him pope, but his

reign didn't last. It was only three days when
he was taken away and led to the scaffold again.
A miracle? No. In Rome, that's how it is.

Qui niera, Gillebert, s'il ne veut résister
Au jugement commun, que le siège de Pierre
Qu'on peut dire à bon droit un paradis en terre,
Aussi bien que le ciel, n'ait son grand Jupiter?

Les Grecs nous ont fait l'un sur Olympe habiter,
Dont souvent dessus nous ses foudres il desserre:
L'autre du Vatican délâche son tonnerre,
Quand quelque roi l'a fait contre lui dépiter.

Du Jupiter céleste un Ganymède on vante,
Le tusque Jupiter en a plus de cinquante:
L'un de nectar s'enivre, et l'autre de bon vin.

De l'aigle l'un et l'autre a la défense prise,
Mais l'un hait les tyrans, l'autre les favorise:
Le mortel en ceci n'est semblable au divin.

Peter's throne, Gillebert, is said to be
heaven on earth. The Greeks had in their skies
great Jupiter. And in Rome we turn our eyes
to the Vatican, where anyone can see

the similarities. Jove sometimes would throw down
his thunderbolts on mankind from a cloud,
as can the pope on kings when they are proud
or annoying enough to cause his face to frown.

Jove, we are told, had his Ganymede to pour
his wine. The pope has fifty young men for
his not dissimilar appetites. In drink,

the god had his nectar, the pope, his wine. But Jove
hated the tyrants the other appears to love.
There is a small but significant difference, I think.

Où que je tourne l'œil, soit vers le Capitole,
Vers les bains d'Antonin ou Dioclétien,
Et si quelque œuvre encor dure plus ancien
De la porte Saint-Paul jusques à Ponte-mole:

Je déteste à part moi ce vieux faucheur, qui vole,
Et le ciel, qui ce tout a réduit en un rien:
Puis songeant que chacun peut répéter le sien,
Je me blâme, et connais que ma complainte est folle.

Aussi serait celui par trop audacieux,
Qui voudrait accuser ou le temps ou les cieux,
Pour voir une médaille ou colonne brisée.

Et qui sait si les cieux referont point leur tour,
Puisque tant de seigneurs nous voyons chacun jour
Bâtir sur la Rotonde et sur le Colisée?

Whenever I look to the Capitoline or to
Hadrian's baths or Diocletian's, or any
monument that survived in Rome these many
centuries, I hate the old Reaper who

robs and destroys, and Heaven that can reduce
grandeur to rubble. But give the devil his due.
I'm a fool, I realize, and impertinent, too,
to protest against Time and even try to accuse

Heaven because of a medal or broken column.
We lose, but then we gain again in the solemn
process of history. No, I do not mock.

Look at these seigneurs, passing here every day,
whose imperial pride is a reason for hope as they
restore and rebuild with the Coliseum's rock.

Je fus jadis Hercule, or Pasquin je me nomme,
Pasquin fable du peuple, et qui fais toutefois
Le même office encor que j'ai fait autrefois,
Vu qu'ores par mes vers tant de monstres j'assomme.

Aussi mon vrai métier, c'est de n'épargner homme,
Mais les vices chanter d'une publique voix:
Et si ne puis encor, quelque fort que je sois,
Surmonter la fureur de cet Hydre de Rome.

J'ai porté sur mon col le grand palais des dieux,
Pour soulager Atlas, qui sous le faix des cieux
Courbait las et recru sa grande échine large.

Ores au lieu du ciel, je porte sur mon dos,
Un gros moine espagnol, qui me froisse les os,
Et me pèse trop plus que ma première charge.

Hercules once, I'm now retitled, demoted:
Pasquino now, but my labors continue the same,
attacking monsters, though using the new name,
and instead of a club it's verse to which I'm devoted.

I call out at the top of my voice, the vice
that everywhere I see, though I cannot win,
for the Hydra of Rome has a repertoire of sin
that's utterly inexhaustible. Once or twice

I've helped out Atlas, holding up on my shoulder
the palace of gods. (He's tired and growing older.)
Now I've an even heavier burden to bear,

a more exhausting and even a daunting mission—
to hold up a monk from the Spanish Inquisition,
who weighs much more than all the gods in the air.

Comme un qui veut curer quelque cloaque immonde,
S'il n'a le nez armé d'une contresenteur,
Étouffé bien souvent de la grand puanteur
Demeure enseveli dans l'ordure profonde:

Ainsi le bon Marcel ayant levé la bonde,
Pour laisser écouler la fangeuse épaisseur
Des vices entassés, dont son prédécesseur
Avait six ans devant empoisonné le monde:

Se trouvant le pauvret de telle odeur surpris,
Tomba mort au milieu de son œuvre entrepris,
N'ayant pas à demi cette ordure purgée.

Mais quiconque rendra tel ouvrage parfait,
Se pourra bien vanter d'avoir beaucoup plus fait
Que celui qui purgea les étables d'Augée.

If you're going to clean out a cesspool, you want to wear
a mask on your nose for protection against the smell.
Some of those who haven't choked and fell
into the shit and drowned and were buried there.

So, when Marcellus opened the drain to let
out the filth that Julius had left behind,
the poor fellow, knocked back by the noxious wind,
collapsed and died, with the job not half done yet.

A dismal story, I fear, but there's reason to hope.
We'll have, in the course of things, another pope,
and he'll have his work cut out for him. Oh, yes.

A heroic labor awaits him, a noble sequel
to what Marcellus did, and more than the equal
of Hercules' job with the Augean stables' mess.

Quand mon Caraciol de leur prison desserre
Mars, les vents et l'hiver: une ardente fureur,
Une fière tempête, une tremblante horreur
Ames, ondes, humeurs, ard, renverse et resserre.

Quand il lui plaît aussi de renfermer la guerre
Et l'orage et le froid: une amoureuse ardeur,
Une longue bonace, une douce tiédeur
Brûle, apaise et résout les cœurs, l'onde et la terre

Ainsi la paix à Mars il oppose en un temps,
Le beau temps à l'orage, à l'hiver le printemps,
Comparant Paule quart avec Jules troisième.

Aussi ne furent onc deux siècles plus divers,
Et ne se peut mieux voir l'endroit par le revers
Que mettant Jules tiers avec Paule quatrième.

When Caracciolo lets loose the wrath of Mars,
or the bitter winds of winter, he makes us see
with our own eyes the violence, and he
can fill our hearts with terror, but when his wars

are over and he is done with the heat and cold
and wants to show us peace and calm, he can,
and our hearts are eased in a vision of God and man
at peace in some harmonious age of gold.

So he can contrast peace and war on a page,
fair weather and storms, or amity and rage,
or Paul the Fourth and Julius the Third, whose two

centuries could not have differed more.
No one could better show what went before
and then what followed, the old and then the new.

Je n'ai jamais pensé que cette voûte ronde
Couvrît rien de constant: mais je veux désormais,
Je veux, mon cher Morel, croire plus que jamais
Que dessous ce grand Tout rien ferme ne se fonde,

Puisque celui qui fut de la terre et de l'onde
Le tonnerre et l'effroi, las de porter le faix,
Veut d'un cloître borner la grandeur de ses faits,
Et pour servir à Dieu abandonner le monde.

Mais quoi? que dirons-nous de cet autre vieillard,
Lequel ayant passé son âge plus gaillard
Au service de Dieu, ores César imite?

Je ne sais qui des deux est le moins abusé:
Mais je pense, Morel, qu'il est fort malaisé
Que l'un soit bon guerrier, ni l'autre bon ermite.

What obtains, Morel? How can this be?
I never supposed that the firmament was very
firm, but I thought there were rules, and now I worry
that nothing makes sense. The man who ruled land and sea

with thunderbolts and terror has retired
to a cloister, has given up the world for God.
But can we call Charles V any more odd
than Paul IV, the pope whom all admired,

and who's turned to the emperor's trade, learning to wage
war as the occupation of his old age?
Are both of them wrong? Or are both of them right? Who
    cares?

Nothing is certain now. We are all confused
by this blurring of all the principles we used
to believe in—and one's warfare and the other's prayers.

Quand je vois ces seigneurs qui l'épée et la lance
Ont laissé pour vêtir ce saint orgueil romain,
Et ceux-là qui ont pris le bâton en la main
Sans avoir jamais fait preuve de leur vaillance:

Quand je les vois, Ursin, si chiches d'audience
Que souvent par quatre huis on la mendie en vain:
Et quand je vois l'orgueil d'un camérier hautain,
Lequel ferait à Job perdre la patience:

Il me souvient alors de ces lieux enchantés
Qui sont en *Amadis* et *Palmerin* chantés,
Desquels l'entrée était si chèrement vendue.

Puis je dis: O combien le palais que je vois
Me semble différent du palais de mon roi,
Où l'on ne trouve point de chambre défendue!

When I see these seigneurs who have let go
the sword and lance to put on the pomp of Rome
and those who have taken in hand the marshal's baton,
never before having held a weapon—for show

and to play at soldiers; Ursin, when I behold
them, much too grand for anyone to approach,
with eighteen antechambers, and in each
a haughty footman, liveried in gold

braid (it would try a Job's patience, I fear);
I think of those palaces of yesteryear—
Amadis, Palmerin, and such as these—

and then of the Papal Palace, a quite different thing
from those I've seen in France, in which the king
keeps his door open: you come and go as you please.

Avoir vu dévaler une triple montagne,
Apparoir une biche et disparoir soudain,
Et dessus le tombeau d'un empereur romain
Une vieille carafe élever pour enseigne:

Ne voir qu'entrer soldats et sortir en campagne,
Emprisonner seigneurs pour un crime incertain,
Retourner forussiz, et le Napolitain
Commander en son rang à l'orgueil de l'Espagne:

Force nouveaux seigneurs, dont les plus apparents
Sont de Sa Sainteté les plus proches parents,
Et force cardinaux, qu'à grand-peine l'on nomme:

Force braves chevaux, et force hauts collets,
Et force favoris, qui n'étaient que valets:
Voilà, mon cher Dagaut, des nouvelles de Rome.

High Monte is brought down; Cervini, too,
his mild successor, like some startled deer,
is laid upon Hadrian's tomb . . . Then what comes here?
Caraffa is presented. What can we do

as soldiers arrive and then depart on campaign?
Great men are in jail for no particular crime;
exiles return again; and all this time,
the pope in Naples is disciplining Spain.

New seigneurs are created every day
(many, the pope's relations, people say);
and cardinals, too, with names nobody knows.

Look at their horses and carriages, so splendid.
(They were mere pages in the month just ended.)
In Rome, my dear Dagaut, that's how it goes.

O trois et quatre fois malheureuse la terre
Dont le prince ne voit que par les yeux d'autrui,
N'entend que par ceux-là qui répondent pour lui,
Aveugle, sourd et mut plus que n'est une pierre!

Tels sont ceux-là, Seigneur, qu'aujourd'hui l'on resserre
Oisifs dedans leur chambre, ainsi qu'en un étui,
Pour durer plus longtemps, et ne sentir l'ennui
Que sent leur pauvre peuple accablé de la guerre.

Ils se paissent enfants de trompes et canons,
De fifres, de tambours, d'enseignes, gonfanons,
Et de voir leur province aux ennemis en proie.

Tel était celui-là, qui du haut d'une tour,
Regardant ondoyer la flamme tout autour,
Pour se donner plaisir chantait le feu de Troie.

O thrice and four times unhappy is that land
whose prince sees only what others see and can hear
only what they hear, as if he were
deaf, blind, and dumb, and could not understand

anything on his own. As bad are these
shut up in their rooms as if in some gift box
that has been devised to protect them from the shocks
of life, the common people's miseries.

They play like little boys with trumpets and cannons,
fifes and drums, and brightly colored pennons,
risking the province carelessly, even with joy.

They are like that king in the tower—what was his name?—
who looked down to see all round him the tongues of flame
and was pleased to think they were much like the fires at
    Troy.

O que tu es heureux, si tu connais ton heur,
D'être échappé des mains de cette gent cruelle,
Qui sous un faux semblant d'amitié mutuelle
Nous dérobe le bien, et la vie, et l'honneur!

Où tu es, mon Dagaut, la secrète rancœur,
Le soin qui comme une hydre en nous se renouvelle,
L'avarice, l'envie, et la haine immortelle
Du chétif courtisan n'empoisonnent le cœur.

La molle oisiveté n'y engendre le vice,
Le serviteur n'y perd son temps et son service,
Et n'y médit-on point de cil qui est absent:

La justice y a lieu, la foi n'en est bannie,
Là ne sait-on que c'est de prendre à compagnie,
A change, à cense, à stock, et à trente pour cent.

My friend, you have no idea how lucky you
have been, to escape from the hands of these cruel men
who pretend that they are our fastest friends but then
steal our money, our lives, and our honor, too.

Where you are, dear Dagaut, there is no spite
hiding itself, no backstabbing or spying,
avarice, envy, or courtier's hate undying
to poison the air you breathe both day and night.

A moment of leisure is not an occasion for vice.
Nobody works without getting paid the price
of his labor. Slander is not a matter of course.

Justice is not unheard of and friendship is not
dangerous. Nobody calculates just what
friendships are worth, as a broker would do on the bourse.

Fuyons, Dilliers, fuyons cette cruelle terre,
Fuyons ce bord avare et ce peuple inhumain,
Que des dieux irrités la vengeresse main
Ne nous accable encor sous un même tonnerre.

Mars est désenchaîné, le temple de la guerre
Est ouvert à ce coup, le grand prêtre romain
Veut foudroyer là-bas l'hérétique Germain
Et l'Espagnol marran, ennemis de saint Pierre.

On ne voit que soldats, enseignes, gonfanons,
On n'oit que tambourins, trompettes et canons,
On ne voit que chevaux courant parmi la plaine:

On n'oit plus raisonner que de sang et de feu,
Maintenant on verra, si jamais on l'a veu,
Comment se sauvera la nacelle romaine.

Let us get out, Dilliers, while we can. Let's fly
at once from this grasping town and inhumane
people, before the furious deities rain
down on our heads their thunderbolts from on high.

Mars is let loose, and the doors of the temple of war
are opened wide, as the high priest of Rome pursues
the German heretics and the Spanish Jews,
those converts—Marranos who pray to God as before.

There are soldiers everywhere, and trumpets and drums.
A platoon marches down one street, and another comes
on horseback up another. The prospects are dark.

All you hear now is the talk of blood and fire,
and how the situation grows ever more dire.
Can the pope, our captain, save the Roman ark?

Celui vraiment était et sage et bien appris,
Qui, connaissant du feu la semence divine
Être des animants la première origine,
De substance de feu dit être nos esprits.

Le corps est le tison de cette ardeur épris,
Lequel, d'autant qu'il est de matière plus fine,
Fait un feu plus luisant, et rend l'esprit plus digne
De montrer ce qui est en soi-même compris.

Ce feu donques céleste, humble de sa naissance,
S'élève peu à peu au lieu de son essence,
Tant qu'il soit parvenu au point de sa grandeur:

Adonc il diminue, et sa force lassée,
Par faute d'aliment en cendres abaissée,
Sent faillir tout à coup sa languissante ardeur.

He was a wise man who first declared
fire to be the divine seed and the source
of life for every creature as well as the force
that animates our spirits, the torch prepared

to energize both the body and the mind.
The finer the fuel, the better it can blaze,
and the quicker can the mind perform displays
of its higher nature to leave the body behind.

This celestial fire that brings us out of the dark
and cold begins with an insignificant spark
and blazes up to achieve its grandeur. Then

having consumed its fuel, it slowly decreases
to a pile of ash, and soon thereafter it ceases.
As fires blaze and die down, so it happens with men.

Quand je vois ces messieurs, desquels l'autorité
Se voit ores ici commander en son rang,
D'un front audacieux cheminer flanc à flanc,
Il me semble de voir quelque divinité.

Mais les voyant pâlir lorsque Sa Sainteté
Crache dans un bassin, et d'un visage blanc
Cautement épier s'il y a point de sang,
Puis d'un petit souris feindre une sûreté:

O combien (dis-je alors) la grandeur que je voy
Est misérable au prix de la grandeur d'un Roi!
Malheureux qui si cher achète tel honneur.

Vraiment le fer meurtrier et le rocher aussi
Pendent bien sur le chef de ces seigneurs ici,
Puisque d'un vieux filet dépend tout leur bonheur.

When I see these powerful men come and go in the hall,
each in his station a man of power and rank,
marching in their impressive phalanx, I think,
in the presence of such demigods, I'm small

and helpless; but then, I see their panic attacks
whenever His Holiness coughs—he's got the catarrh—
and they peek into the basin to see if there are
flecks of blood . . . No? They can smile and relax.

How fragile is all this grandeur compared to a king's,
and how little safety all this honor brings
with the sword of Damocles hanging over your head—

or a huge rock that at any moment could fall,
demolishing everything, ruining one and all.
Their grandeur, their power, their lives hang by a thread.

Brusquet à son retour vous racontera, Sire,
De ces rouges prélats la pompeuse apparence,
Leurs mules, leurs habits, leur longue révérence,
Qui se peut beaucoup mieux représenter que dire.

Il vous racontera, s'il les sait bien décrire,
Les mœurs de cette cour, et quelle différence
Se voit de ces grandeurs à la grandeur de France,
Et mille autres bons points, qui sont dignes de rire.

Il vous peindra la forme et l'habit du Saint Père,
Qui comme Jupiter tout le monde tempère,
Avecques un clin d'œil: sa faconde et sa grâce,

L'honnêteté des siens, leur grandeur et largesse,
Les présents qu'on lui fit, et de quelle caresse
Tout ce que se dit vôtre à Rome l'on embrasse.

Brusquet will tell you, Your Majesty, how grand
these prelates are with their slippers, their bright red
    flowing
robes, the elaborate bows they make, coming and going . . .
He'll do them for you, performing at your command.

He'll tell you how it is at this court and what
the difference is between France's grandeur and this,
and will he make you laugh, describing how it is
and what the Holy Father is like who with but

a blink of his eye can change the world at his whim.
The manners of all the men attending him
he'll recount for you, and the bribes, or call them gifts.

He'll explain to you all the intricacies that here
govern the court and tell you who has the ear
of whom and who gets the longer or shorter shrifts.

Voici le carnaval, menons chacun la sienne,
Allons baller en masque, allons nous promener,
Allons voir Marc Antoine ou Zany bouffonner
Avec son Magnifique à la vénitienne:

Voyons courir le pal à la mode ancienne,
Et voyons par le nez le sot buffle mener:
Voyons le fier taureau d'armes environner,
Et voyons au combat l'adresse italienne:

Voyons d'œufs parfumés un orage grêler,
Et la fusée ardent siffler menu par l'air.
Sus donc, dépêchons-nous, voici la pardonnance:

Il nous faudra demain visiter les saints lieux,
Là nous ferons l'amour, mais ce sera des yeux,
Car passer plus avant, c'est contre l'ordonnance.

It's Carnival! Let us each find a girl and go
to the masked ball to promenade in the streets,
look at the jesters and clowns perform their feats,
and observe as the great men who see the show

in which they're made fun of have to maintain a smile.
Let's watch the water buffalo led by the nose,
the bullfights, the soldiers who put on their martial shows,
and the footraces they run in the ancient style.

Let's laugh as they fling a shower of rotten eggs,
or set off fireworks from their powder kegs,
and enjoy as much as we can this dispensation

from all restraint. Tomorrow, after sunrise,
if we make love it can only be with our eyes.
Any more than that would break the regulation.

Se fâcher tout le jour d'une fâcheuse chasse,
Voir un brave taureau se faire un large tour,
Étonné de se voir tant d'hommes alentour,
Et cinquante piquiers affronter son audace:

Le voir en s'élançant venir la tête basse,
Fuir et retourner d'un plus brave retour,
Puis le voir à la fin pris en quelque détour,
Percé de mille coups, ensanglanter la place:

Voir courir aux flambeaux, mais sans se rencontrer,
Donner trois coups d'épée, en armes se montrer,
Et tout autour du camp un rempart de Tudesques:

Dresser un grand apprêt, faire attendre longtemps,
Puis donner à la fin un maigre passe-temps:
Voilà tout le plaisir des fêtes romanesques.

To be driven mad the whole day long in a mad
sport, and to see a brave bull in that ring,
harassed, tormented, the poor enormous thing
worn down by the pricks of picadors . . . It's sad.

He puts his head down and charges, and once more
backs off and charges again, bellowing, game,
but doomed, for in the end, it is always the same,
with his powerful body streaming blood and gore

as costumed functionaries here and there
run, waving smoky torches in the air,
and, from the crowd, there comes an animal noise

that drowns out that of the bull. The matador strikes.
This is what they came for, what the crowd likes.
This is what the discerning Roman enjoys.

Cependant qu'au palais de procès tu devises,
D'avocats, procureurs, présidents, conseillers,
D'ordonnances, d'arrêts, de nouveaux officiers,
De juges corrompus, et de telles surprises:

Nous devisons ici de quelques villes prises,
De nouvelles de banque, et de nouveaux courriers,
De nouveaux cardinaux, de mules, d'estafiers,
De chapes, de rochets, de masses et valises:

Et ores, Sibilet, que je t'écris ceci,
Nous parlons de taureaux, et de buffles aussi,
De masques, de banquets, et de telles dépenses:

Demain nous parlerons d'aller aux stations,
De motu-proprio, de réformations,
D'ordonnances, de brefs, de bulles et dispenses.

Where you are in the Palace, all the news
is of lawsuits, barristers, proctors, chancery cases,
solicitors, referees, with old and young faces,
and corrupt judges (what other kind would they choose?).

Here the talk is of petty triumphs in which
bankers prosper, or cardinals are made,
or of shoes and robes and uniforms with gold braid,
of masses, and of nonentities suddenly rich.

And no less important, Sibilet, as I write
are the bullfights in the daytime and then, at night,
the banquets, masques, and similar recreations.

Tomorrow it will be of processions to shrines,
and pieces of parchment covered in spidery lines,
and ordinances, bulls, bills, and dispensations.

» 123

Nous ne sommes fâchés que la trêve se fasse:
Car bien que nous soyons de la France bien loin,
Si est chacun de nous à soi-même témoin
Combien la France doit de la guerre être lasse.

Mais nous sommes fâchés que l'espagnole audace,
Qui plus que le Français de repos a besoin,
Se vante avoir la guerre et la paix en son poing,
Et que de respirer nous lui donnons espace.

Il nous fâche d'ouïr nos pauvres alliés
Se plaindre à tous propos qu'on les ait oubliés,
Et qu'on donne au privé l'utilité commune.

Mais ce qui plus nous fâche est que les étrangers
Disent plus que jamais que nous sommes légers,
Et que nous ne savons connaître la fortune.

We are not sorry there's been a truce. Though far
away for all these years from France, we know
this brings relief to a nation wearied so
by the unremitting burdens of waging war.

Still it's distressing that Spain in its insolence,
and needing the respite as much as we do or more,
can claim that it decides between peace and war
to suit itself, and the choice is not that of France.

We regret what our beleaguered allies have suffered
and their complaints about how our policies differed,
although we're united, with interests that still coincide.

Most of all we regret what foreigners say—
that we're frivolous and we always behave this way,
and cannot recognize Fortune or history's tide.

Le roi (disent ici ces bannis de Florence)
Du sceptre d'Italie est frustré désormais,
Et son heureuse main cet heur n'aura jamais
De reprendre aux cheveux la fortune de France.

Le Pape mal content n'aura plus de fiance
En tous ces beaux desseins trop légèrement faits,
Et l'exemple siennois rendra par cette paix
Suspecte aux étrangers la française alliance.

L'Empereur affaibli ses forces reprendra,
L'Empire héréditaire à ce coup il rendra,
Et paisible à ce coup il rendra l'Angleterre.

Voilà que disent ceux qui discourent du roi.
Que leur répondrons-nous? Vineus, mande-le moi,
Toi, qui sais discourir et de paix et de guerre.

The king, the Florentine exiles claim, will never
clutch in his hand the scepter of Italy
or even restore France's good fortune, for he
has lost the trust of the pope with all those clever

stratagems he proclaims and then retracts.
Foreigners who remember Siena and how
he behaved will be afraid to trust him now
or make with the French alliances or pacts.

The emperor, weak now, will recover his force,
and his empire will survive and thrive of course,
while England will stay at peace as it was before.

When people speak these days of our king and nation,
that's what they're saying, Vineus. And what refutation
do you propose, as an expert on peace and war?

Dedans le ventre obscur, où jadis fut enclos
Tout cela qui depuis a rempli ce grand vide,
L'air, la terre, et le feu, et l'élément liquide,
Et tout cela qu'Atlas soutient dessus son dos,

Les semences du Tout étaient encore en gros,
Le chaud avec le sec, le froid avec l'humide,
Et l'accord, qui depuis leur imposa la bride,
N'avait encore ouvert la porte du chaos:

Car la guerre en avait la serrure brouillée,
Et la clef en était par l'âge si rouillée
Qu'en vain, pour en sortir, combattait ce grand corps,

Sans la trêve, Seigneur, de la paix messagère,
Qui trouva le secret, et d'une main légère
La paix avec l'amour en fit sortir dehors.

» 125

In that dark belly in which once was confined
all that since filled the universal void,
the air, earth, fire, and water were not yet alloyed
to make up Atlas's load. And still combined

were hot and dry and cold and wet. The laws
of science had not been thought of yet or set
down, and the Gate of Chaos was still shut.
One might have looked to War to find the cause

as if it had filled the lock with grit, and Age
had somehow rusted the key. And at that stage
the fetus struggled but could not work free

without a truce, Seigneur. But then, with the peace,
it could at last effectuate a release,
and order emerged with love's facility.

Tu sois la bienvenue, ô bienheureuse trêve!
Trêve que le chrétien ne peut assez chanter,
Puisque seule tu as la vertu d'enchanter
De nos travaux passés la souvenance grève.

Tu dois durer cinq ans: et que l'envie en crève:
Car si le ciel bénin te permet enfanter
Ce qu'on attend de toi, tu te pourras vanter
D'avoir fait une paix qui ne sera si brève.

Mais si le favori en ce commun repos
Doit avoir désormais le temps plus à propos
D'accuser l'innocent, pour lui ravir sa terre:

Si le fruit de la paix du peuple tant requis
A l'avare avocat est seulement acquis:
Trêve, va-t'en en paix, et retourne la guerre.

Most welcome are you, O truce, bringing relief
of which, as Christians, we cannot sing the praise
loudly enough: you enchant us and erase
all memory of our hardship and our grief.

You're supposed to last five years, as I hope you shall.
If through the grace of heaven you can achieve
what you intend, then we may perhaps believe
that we may enjoy those years of peace that all

desire. But if one party, with every reason
to be content, should balk somehow or seize on
the chance to accuse and complain and invade as before,

then all those people now celebrating the peace,
finding themselves worse off than before, will cease
their hymns of thanks and pray once more for war.

Ici de mille fards la traïson se déguise,
Ici mille forfaits pullulent à foison,
Ici ne se punit l'homicide ou poison,
Et la richesse ici par usure est acquise:

Ici les grands maisons viennent de bâtardise,
Ici ne se croit rien sans humaine raison,
Ici la volupté est toujours de saison,
Et d'autant plus y plaît que moins elle est permise.

Pense le demeurant. Si est-ce toutefois
Qu'on garde encore ici quelque forme de lois,
Et n'en est point du tout la justice bannie.

Ici le grand seigneur n'achète l'action,
Et pour priver autrui de sa possession
N'arme son mauvais droit de force et tyrannie.

Here treason assumes a thousand disguises;
here are more monstrous crimes than one's mind conceives
and nobody's punished, not homicides or thieves,
or usurers with wealth no one penalizes.

Here great houses are founded by bastards; here
no one has faith except in human reason.
In pursuit of pleasure, here always in season,
what's forbidden pleases all the more, I fear.

The rest is what you'd imagine. But sometimes,
some forms of law remain in effect. Some crimes
are disapproved of. Justice can run its course—

when a grand seigneur cannot suborn his way
to the verdict he wants from judges in his pay
or frighten the courts with a threat of naked force.

Ce n'est pas de mon gré, Carle, que ma navire
Erre en la mer tyrrhène: un vent impétueux
La chasse malgré moi par ces flots tortueux,
Ne voyant plus le pol, qui sa faveur t'inspire.

Je ne vois que rochers, et si rien se peut dire
Pire que des rochers le heurt audacieux:
Et le phare jadis favorable à mes yeux
De mon cours égaré sa lanterne retire.

Mais si je puis un jour me sauver des dangers
Que je fuis vagabond par ces flots étrangers,
Et voir de l'océan les campagnes humides,

J'arrêterai ma nef au rivage gaulois,
Consacrant ma dépouille au Neptune françois,
A Glauque, à Mélicerte, et aux sœurs Néréides.

It isn't my idea, Carle, going by boat
across the sea where impetuous winds may blow
you off course or the tides defy you. And as you know
there's nothing of interest to see but some rocks of note—

because of the ships that went down nearby. On shore
were beacons mariners hoped for on watch in the dark
to determine where they were in the voyage and mark
their position, but sailors report they're not there anymore.

And if someday I can save myself from these dangers
and cross these seas that are traveled by reckless strangers
to behold instead an ocean of waving grass,

I will draw up my vessel at last on some Gallic strand
and offer my kit to the gods—the French Neptune, and
Glaucus, and maybe some nice Nereid lass.

Je vois, Dilliers, je vois seréner la tempête,
Je vois le vieux Protée son troupeau renfermer,
Je vois le vert Triton s'égayer sur la mer,
Et vois l'astre jumeau flamboyer sur ma tête:

Jà le vent favorable à mon retour s'apprête,
Jà vers le front du port je commence à ramer,
Et vois jà tant d'amis que ne les puis nommer,
Tendant les bras vers moi, sur le bord faire fête.

Je vois mon grand Ronsard, je le connais d'ici,
Je vois mon cher Morel, et mon Dorat aussi,
Je vois mon de La Haye, et mon Paschal encore:

Et vois un peu plus loin (si je ne suis déçu)
Mon divin Mauléon, duquel, sans l'avoir vu,
La grâce, le savoir et la vertu j'adore.

I see, Dilliers, the storm is subsiding; I see
Proteus shut up his savage troop and green
Triton frolicking on the waves. I've seen
Castor and Pollux blaze overhead. Home free,

with a fair wind behind me, I row into port.
There, on the dock, I can see my good friends waiting,
waving, holding their arms out, celebrating.
The great Ronsard, I can make out at this short

distance, and there's Morel, and Dorat, I do
believe, and Delahaie and, yes, Paschal, too,
if I'm not deceived. A little farther off,

I can make out my divine Mauleon's face.
I've never seen him before, but that learning, that grace,
that virtue I've long admired, I know well enough.

Et je pensais aussi ce que pensait Ulysse,
Qu'il n'était rien plus doux que voir encore un jour
Fumer sa cheminée, et après long séjour
Se retrouver au sein de sa terre nourrice.

Je me réjouissais d'être échappé au vice,
Aux Circés d'Italie, aux sirènes d'amour,
Et d'avoir rapporté en France à mon retour
L'honneur que l'on s'acquiert d'un fidèle service.

Las, mais après l'ennui de si longue saison,
Mille soucis mordants je trouve en ma maison,
Qui me rongent le cœur sans espoir d'allégeance.

Adieu donques, Dorat, je suis encor romain,
Si l'arc que les neuf Sœurs te mirent en la main
Tu ne me prête ici, pour faire ma vengeance.

And I have thought what Ulysses must have thought—
that nothing could be sweeter than once more
to see the smoke curl up as it did before
from the chimney of that house in which I was brought

up. I rejoiced for having escaped the lewd
Italian Circes and Sirens who walk the street
in Rome, and hoped that in France again, I'd meet
the honor that ought to accrue to years of good

service. But I was wrong. My cares in Rome
were less severe than these I find at home,
from which I have no hope of any relief.

Therefore, adieu, Dorat. I'm shipping out
again, unless you teach me to write about
my troubles and make an art form out of my grief.

» Translator's Notes

(Numbers below correspond to poem numbers.)

To Monsieur d'Avanson: Jean de Saint-Marcel, seigneur d'Avanson, was a member of the Privy Council and a protégé of Marguerite of France. Du Bellay's friend Olivier Magny served for a time as his secretary.

1 It is assumed that the immediate prompting for this sonnet was the publication in 1556 of the *Hymnes* of Pierre de Ronsard.

2 Pierre de Paschal, a friend of Ronsard and the Pléiade poets, was a historian and courtier.

4 Petrarch, or Francesco Petrarca (1304–74), was the great humanist and poet whose sonnets of the *Canzoniere* were a model not only for Italian literature but for all of Renaissance Europe; Pierre de Ronsard (1524–85), the best known of the Pléiade, was court poet to Charles IX. His work was at first lyric and then he turned to the grand manner to which du Bellay here refers.

7 Marguerite de France (1523–74), Duchess of Savoy, was sister of King Henri II at whose court she had great influence.

10 Ovid, relegated by Augustus Caesar to Tomis, on the Black Sea, wrote the *Tristia* there and complained of the savages who spoke neither Latin nor Greek but Sarmatian and Getic.

12 Olivier Magny (1529?–61) was secretary first to the poet and humanist Hugues Salel and then to d'Avanson, whom he accompanied to Rome.

14 Abbé Étienne Boucher was secretary to the French ambassador to Rome in the 1550s and became Bishop of Quimper in 1560.

15 Jean de Pardeillan de Panjas was secretary to Cardinal Georges d'Armagnac in Rome and was a poet who wrote in both French and Latin. He was associated with both Ronsard and Olivier Magny.

18 Jean de Morel d'Embrun was a humanist attached to the court of Henri II. A doctor and amateur poet, he was a friend of du Bellay.

19 This sonnet is addressed to Ronsard and refers to his *Franciade,* the hero of which is Francus, who is described as an heir of Hector.

21 The reference in the last line is to the painter François Clouet (c. 1510–c. 1572), also called Janet or Jehannet, who inherited his father's position and served as court painter successively under François I, Henri II, François II, and Charles IX.

23 Roland appears in Ariosto's *Orlando Furioso.*

24 Jean-Antoine de Baïf (1532–89) was du Bellay's fellow student at the Collège de Coqueret and was one of the Pléiade. He wrote sonnets, didactic and satirical poems, and plays.

26 Actually, Ronsard was two years younger than du Bellay.

28 Robert Lahaye was a counselor to Parlement and a friend of poets.

30 Louis Bailleul was du Bellay's friend and guide to the Roman ruins.

35 Dillier (or Dilliers or d'Illier) was a friend of du Bellay, Ronsard, and Magny.

42 Jérôme Della Rovere, sieur de Vineus, was an envoy sent by Henri II to Rome in 1556 and 1557. He became Bishop of Toulon in 1559.

50 Scipio Africanus retired to his villa.

51 This is probably Matheiu de Mauny, a clerk in Cardinal du Bellay's staff.

52 The consensus is that this sonnet is addressed to Cardinal du Bellay.

53 Jean-Antoine de Simiane Gordes was seigneur de Cabanis and an apostolic protonotary. He and du Bellay were close friends.

54 Charles Maraud (or Marault) was valet de chambre of Cardinal du Bellay.

55 Montigné has not been identified but, obviously, was connected in some way with the law.

57 Dagaut, obviously a friend back in France, is otherwise unknown, except for his mention in 113. Nicolas Le Breton was secretary to Cardinal du Bellay. The poet reproached him for having copied and clandestinely circulated around Rome some of the sonnets of *The Regrets,* an action which caused the author some difficulty.

59 Pierre was du Bellay's barber in Rome.

60 Du Bellay is referring to his "Epitaph for a Cat," one of the poems in his *Jeux Rustiques*.

63 Charles de l'Estrange was protonotary of Cardinal de Guise. He died in 1565.

64 The sonnet may be addressed to Claude de Bizé, whom du Bellay knew in Paris and who later became canon at Notre-Dame de Paris, or it may be that the person addressed is d'Odoard Bizet, secretary of François de Guise in Italy.

66 Denis the Younger, Tyrant of Syracuse, became a schoolmaster after he was exiled.

71 Rémi Belleau (1528–77) was one of the Pléiade poets.

72 Jacques Gohory was a philosopher, scholar, and translator and a friend in Paris of Magny and of du Bellay.

78 Jacques Peletier (or Pelletier) du Mans (1517–82) was a poet, mathematician, and philologist who, with du Bellay, was an advocate of writing in the vernacular French rather than in Latin.

82 Jean Duthier (or du Thier), seigneur de Beauregard, was counselor to the king and secretary of state. He was a protector of poets and a friend to du Bellay.

83 Florimond Robertet, baron of Alluye, was a friend of Ronsard and, through family connections, was influential at court.

90 Jacques Bouju (1515–77) was from Anjou, a friend both of du Bellay and of Ronsard. He was a magistrate and a poet both in Latin and in French.

91 This is—need one say?—a parody of the Petrarchan love sonnet.

97 Rémy Doulcin, priest, doctor, and clerk of the diocese of Chartres.

100 The Ursin to whom this sonnet is addressed could be Charles Juvénal des Ursan, Cardinal du Bellay's chaplain, or it could be the humanist Fluvio Orsini, or perhaps an Italian Captain P. G. Orsini who served the French.

101 Melin (or Mellin) de Saint-Gelais (1491–1558) studied in Italy and was then almoner and, later, librarian to Henri II. He became Bishop of Angoulême. He was at first critical of the Pléiade but came over to be one of their supporters. He was one of the first to write sonnets in French.

103 Cardinal Carlo Caraffa (1519–61) had as his Ganymede a certain Ascagne (or Ascaigne). Ascanius was the son of Aeneas. Aeneas's mother was, of course, Venus, which made him half brother to Cupid.

104 The pope of whom du Bellay writes here is Julius III, who died in 1555.

105 In 1550 Julius III made a seventeen-year-old boy a cardinal.

106 Pierre Gillebert (or Gilebert, or Gilbert) was a counselor to the Parlement of Grenoble, a poet who wrote in Latin, and a friend of Magny, whom he visited·in Rome.

108 The statue to which du Bellay refers was originally thought to be of Hercules but was then reidentified as Pasquino. Satires—or pasquinades—were posted on it.

109 Marcellus II, who succeeded Julius III, was a man of virtue but his reign as pope lasted only twenty-one days.

110 Jean-Antoine Caracciolo, Bishop of Troyes, came to Rome in 1555 to try, unsuccessfully, to get a cardinal's hat. He was a poet in French, Latin, and Italian, and one of his compositions compared Popes Julius III and Paul IV.

113 The Monte refers to Pope Julius III, who was a del Monte; Marcel II was a Cervini, and Paul IV was a Caraffa.

119 Jean-Antoine Lombard, called Brusquet, was buffon to François I, Henri II, François II, and Charles IX. He visited Rome in 1557 in the entourage of the Cardinal of Lorraine.

122 Thomas Sibilet (or perhaps Sébillet) was an advocate at the Parlement of Paris and author, in 1548, of *Art poétique*, a book critical of du Bellay. They were later reconciled.

123 The Truce of Vaucelle of February 5, 1556, between Henri II and Charles V, is the subject of this sonnet. News of the truce arrived at Rome ten days after the truce was declared. Two months earlier, the Vatican had concluded an alliance with France against Spain, and this arrangement was considered to be a betrayal of that prior agreement.

128 Lancelot de Carle (1500–68), Bishop of Riez, undertook many diplomatic missions to Italy. He was a translator and a poet in French, Latin, and Italian and was highly esteemed by the Pléiade.